THE CALLING OF THE BRIDE
An Intimate Journey
Toward the Heart of God

Dr. Judith Moore

Published by CSA Publishing
A department of Christian Services Association
P.O. Box 1017
Maricopa, Arizona 85139
Unites States of America
www.XPpublishing.com

ISBN 978 -1-936101-63-4

CSA
PUBLISHING

ENDORSEMENTS

As I have grown to know Judith over the years, I have always been impressed with her biblical knowledge. She latches onto a subject that interests her and studies it tenaciously, digging unto the Scriptures, until she receives deep revelation that most of us overlook. *The Calling of the Bride* is the result of such study, prayer and meditation. Anyone who takes the time to read and digest the revelation found in this book will be blessed. "And the Spirit and the bride say, Come." Revelation 22:17 Let those who have ears to hear, listen carefully to what the Spirit says.

Dr. Marilyn Hargis
Founder & President
Gateway To Glory Ministries

Dr. Judith Moore follows the passage from Luke 22:14-20, with this statement, "The celebration of communion is the celebration of INTIMACY with our spiritual Bridegroom." Over and over she speaks of intimacy with the Lord and INSPIRES us to get serious about our preparation as the BRIDE OF CHRIST!

Dr. Moore gives some enlightening comparisons of the Old Testament espousal that proceeded the consummation of marriage. Her statement concerning the bride's acceptance of the proposal of marriage is most moving:

"If she drank from the cup, the marriage
was sealed and they became legally married.
He would then say to her I will not drink of this
cup until we are reunited."

These thoughts encourage us to "DRINK FROM THE CUP" and dedicate ourselves more and more, in serious preparation for an intimate - ongoing relationship with our Lord and Bridegroom.

Dr. George and Bishop Clarice Fluitt
Founders: The Eagles Nest Church and Training Center
Monroe, Louisiana

I was moved and inspired reading the book. Truly Judith Moore has brought to light wonderful details in her writing and loving thoughts of the Scripture. God gave us so much to learn and I feel she captures insights and gives glory to God in the writing. She is a special child of God and a joy to know as a Sister in Christ.

Gwynette Palmer
Sister in the Lord

If I were to write something, it would be to recommend your book based on my life-long admiration of my big sister and her faith in the Lord, evidenced by the life she has lived, the love she has shown, and the inspiration she has been to me as well as to many, many people whom God has brought across her path. I believe you do know intimacy with the Lord on a deeper level than most, and I hope and pray you will continue your "dance with Him"!!

Love you always and forever,

Jane Elledge
Sister

DEDICATION
of my book to
UDEMA MOORE

I would like to dedicate this book in memory and honor of my mother, Udema Moore. (1921-2004) Her wonderful example throughout my life was one that exemplified a Christian woman. Her quiet faith always spoke volumes to me. She was such a sincere woman of God that I wanted to pattern my own life after because she always had something kind to say and shared her Christian love and faith with others as well as her own family. How thankful I have always been to have such a wonderful Mom that loved the Lord. She was my best friend that I could always confide in and I respected her for that attribute. She always had a word of encouragement no matter what the situation.

Words cannot express what is on my heart regarding how much she has always meant in my life. All I can say is "thanks Mom for all you imparted into my life – you were always a blessing and my hero!"

Also, I want to dedicate this book in glory to God and for Jesus, my Beloved Friend, that gave His life for me in order that I might be His Bride. Thank you, Jesus!

Judith

TABLE OF CONTENTS

FOREWORD

This is a Must-Read book for anyone who desires a more intimate relationship with the Lord.

You will feel the Lord pulling you into His Arms of Love as you carefully study the depth of the truths, which the Holy Spirit has given to Judith.

These truths will not interest the average Christian who is content with living the usual worldly-life. But, for those who are "in love" with their Heavenly Bridegroom, and desire a deeper walk with God, I can highly recommend it. Every page will make you stop and think.

Judith is a quiet, unassuming person, whom I have known for many years. She is always ready to come down to Engeltal (the headquarters of the End-Time Handmaidens and Servants) and lend a helping hand; and when she told me she had written a book, I certainly didn't expect the manuscript that she gave me to read. This is her first book, but I truly believe that if she wrote fifty more books she couldn't go deeper, nor rise higher in the revelation of how the Bride of Christ must make herself ready for her Wedding Day.

There will be many souls at the Marriage Supper of the Lamb, but only those who have "made themselves ready" will be His Bride. If you desire to be more than a guest I recommend that you read and study this book that was not really written by Judith, but by THE TEACHER, THE HOLY SPIRIT.

Gwen R. Shaw,
End-Time Handmaidens, Founder and President

INTRODUCTION

The Lord spoke to my heart one day in regard to the Bride of Christ, and I felt He was saying, "Out of the world, I have called the nations, out of those nations, I have been calling the church; and out of the church at this hour, I am now calling My Bride." We are soon going into the "Bridal Age" and leaving the "Church Age." This journey will be toward the very heart of God. If you have a passion for the Lord Jesus Christ and His intimacy and if you long to know what the Father is looking for in producing a Bride for His Son, then this book is for you.

The Lord Jesus Christ is soon to return for His Bride. It is a Bride that has been pre-determined and a Bride that is appropriate for Him. The perception in the mind of much of the Church is that this Bride will consist of all believers. It is believed by many that the Bride will encompass the entire Body of Christ. Is this an accurate perception? As you will become aware in reading this book, I am convinced that the Bride it is not the entire Body of Christ.

There are many aspects to the "Bride of Christ" and this will just cover some of them. This book will not only describe "The Bride" but will also give you information that involves the significance of how to be a part of that vital aspect of the Body of Christ. Many of you will be intrigued and interested by the title *The Calling of the Bride ~ An intimate journey toward the heart of God.*

This is a very important study for the born-again believer. The reason is this: Whether you are taken or left behind in the soon coming rapture, that aspect of the Bride of Christ, will depend on how you answer to what the Scriptures say about the Bride. We are going to investigate a number of Scriptures about the Bridal Company and/or the Bride of Christ and what those Scriptures are saying to each of us. It is taught by some that all those who are born again are a part of the Bride of Christ. The Lord has directed me to a number of passages that suggest that being born again alone does not entitle just anyone to be in the Bridal Company. Please note that this is not speaking about salvation, or who will spend eternity with Jesus, but rather the role and rewards and blessings of being one who prepares as the "The Bride of Christ."

Together, we will investigate and study Scriptures that talk about who the Bride is . . . and who the Bride is not . . . and many different aspects about how the Bride makes herself ready. We are going to look at what the Bible says about the select group of believers that will be taken away, raptured from this earth, when the Bridegroom Himself, Jesus Christ, comes to get His Bride sometime very soon! This is the Bridal Company who is eagerly awaiting her Bridegroom to come and to take her away.

Why I Wrote This Book

It has always been of deep interest in my heart and mind about the Bride of Christ. I knew that this study was very important in the Body of Christ and was probably written just for me to take in all the benefits of studying this specific subject. It is a subject that I longed to know more about, and I knew others would benefit from it as well. Deep down, I really wanted a more personal and intimate walk in the Lord; and I knew that this study would assist me in this endeavor. There are many differing viewpoints and interpretations when it comes to studying the Bride of Christ. There are many revelations that seem to be around and I did not want this to be just another book. That is why I did not want to write this book; but I knew in my spirit that to satisfy my own hunger and desire, I needed to write about my own longing to make myself ready to be His Bride.

We are in the generation that is seeing revelation from the Word of God come alive more than ever before; and the more we study, the more it is unlocked and disclosed. We will see more imparted to those that are seeking with a pure heart. This may be a book that could be perceived by some people as just another person's opinion, but it is much more than that. My prayer is that you will see some revelations you have never seen before as you study this subject throughout this book.

In my studying, I have come to the conclusion that not everyone who is born again will be raptured as the Bride of Christ! You have the choice to draw your own conclusions regarding this subject. This particular book will primarily deal with the issues of who the Bride is and how to ensure that we are a part of that select group of believers. Whether you can receive and agree with all of my views is not the major concern. The question is this: Do you desire to be included as the Bride of Christ and are you preparing now to be that Bride? It does not matter that you have been pre-, mid- or post-tribulation in your eschatological mind-set, but my purpose is to have each of us know the necessity of understanding of "The Bride of Christ" . . . and my desire is for you to have a new love affair with Jesus and know that intimacy in a deeper way.

Everything that I write in regard to "The Bride of Christ" may or may not prove to be absolutely correct in every detail. Please keep in mind 1 Corinthians 13:12 that says we **"see through a glass darkly"** and **"now I know in part."** I just want to help others see their eternal destiny in light of who they are as a part of the Bridal Company, sharing with Him that intimate relationship as His Bride.

My study of the Bride of Christ has opened up my understanding to many prophetic passages of Scripture! I was able to see the complete meanings of some of the original Greek words (in the New Testament) or Hebrew words (in the Old Testament). Sometimes, this requires deep digging in the wells of information – concordances, different study Bibles, etc. Often in my studies, there has been a second word or definition of a Hebrew or Greek word, not chosen by the Bible translators, that has brought out a prophetic insight into a specific verse that has proven to be significant. It is a delight to study the Word of God and see how the Lord puts all this together to bring glory and honor to Him. There are times it seems like a lot of work, but as my mother used to say, "To do things you love or for those you love, turns work into play and duty into privilege." This study has been a privilege to do for the Kingdom of God and for the glory of God.

One final thing that contributed to an immense amount of illumination and interpretation is that the Lord has shown me that many passages of Scripture have more than one application. This was an eye-opener because this truth is pointed out in Job 11:6: "And that he would show thee the secrets of wisdom, that they are double to that which is!" Look at the word "secrets" – The unsearchable depths of God's wisdom in dealing with all His creatures. Now, let's look at "double" – that the secrets are far greater (the word double being used indefinitely for manifold, or plentiful) than that which is manifested. The secret wisdom of God is infinitely greater than that which is revealed to us by His Word or works: the greatest part of what is known of God, is the least part of those perfections that are in Him.

I had never seen that verse before, but I felt it certainly did apply to my subject about the Bride of Christ. There are many verses that show us what is really in His heart, especially concerning the Bride; and we will never exhaust all the wealth of the Scriptures. We must be willing to study and open our heart to His truths from His Word.

The Principal Goal of this Book

It is important for me to place a reminder here that hopefully will help you to resist the impulse to prejudge whether I am right or wrong without thoroughly studying the contents of this entire book. As I said before, getting you to agree with my eschatological position is not the goal of this book. The principal goal is to exhort all believers, regardless of when they believe the rapture will occur, to be ready and most importantly to be in The Bridal Company of Jesus!

Having said that, you will find out that I am still for the most part, pre-tribulation in my beliefs. However, I now believe that Scripture gives compelling testimony and evidence that only the part of the church that qualifies as the Bride will go in that soon-to-occur rapture that will precede the tribulation. I also believe that Scripture indicates that there is a second rapture for those that are left behind and all those that they will lead to the Lord during the shortened tribulation. What the Word of God says about the succession of events that happen during and after the tribulation is not the main focus of this book.

Considering the Complete Puzzle

Let me share an analogy. The study of end-time prophecy or events through these past few months has been like putting together a 1,000 piece jig-saw puzzle; without the benefit of seeing the completed picture on the box top to use as a guide. The pre-tribulation rapture people have seen many Scriptures fit together that gives a picture that indicates that the rapture will happen before the tribulation begins. Considering that these verses from the Bible fit together so well, they have assumed that they are looking at the completed puzzle. By the same token, post-tribulation and pre-wrath rapture people have seen many Scriptures that seem to fit together leading them to believe that they are seeing the whole picture.

The reality is that they are both seeing part of the picture, but missing the whole picture that the entire Bible paints. Many are like the little boy watching a parade through a knothole in the fence – they only see part of the picture. Yet, when someone helps and lifts this little lad up so he can see over the fence, he will have a more complete picture of the parade. We have been taught for so long that we don't have a view of the entire parade. May this book lift you to new heights, and help you to see more from God's perspective so that you can catch a glimpse of His bigger picture!

In some ways, those that are pre-tribulation, post-tribulation and pre-wrath are all right! I am convinced from Scriptures throughout the Bible that there is a pre-tribulation rapture of the Bride and a second rapture of the tribulation saints on the day of the Lord that would fit the latter two positions. The second rapture would be both post-tribulation in that it would be after a shortened tribulation, and at the same time this second rapture would also be pre-wrath, evacuating the remainder of the church that has been left before the wrath of God falls. We must read God's Word with an open heart and mind if we are to hear what He is telling our spirit.

If you disagree with something you read, place it on the back burner . . . and keep on reading. There will be a time you might want to come back to that point of view. The sole purpose of this writing is to get all believers to see how vitally important it is for them to have a sense of destiny, change their priorities, and become so intimate with Jesus while there is still time remaining before He comes very soon for His Bridal Company.

These are exciting days to be alive! This is God's Kairos time and His time is *now* for the Bride to arise. As never before, now is the time for the Bride of Christ to arise, ablaze with the fire of Holy Passion for our Heavenly Bridegroom. We will become the Bride Jesus longs for, a Bride without spot or blemish. We will be a Bride conformed to His image, doing mighty exploits in His name and His power. We shall be a Bride that will establish His Kingdom, not ours, on earth as it is in Heaven.

We are consumed with desire to become His Bride in a depth of relationship we have never experienced. Let us be carriers of His Glory to such an extent that people can see His glory in our lives.

Honor and reward are at the heart of the matter which will determine who from among Christ's body will be a part of the Bride and who will not. God does not bestow honor lightly. One must be worthy to receive the honor of the Father. Salvation is a free gift, but reward and honor are according to our deeds according to the Scriptures. To be a part of the Bride of Christ is to receive the highest honor. The Bride is given an intimate entrance to the Bridegroom; the two will become one. This honor, however, is not given freely. It is kept for those whose hearts beat with a passion for the Lord Jesus Christ. It is reserved for those who have allowed the finished work of the cross to bring a cleansing and separation in their lives, removing that which is flesh and making it holy. The completed work is done.

Remember what it says in John 19:30, **"When Jesus therefore had received the vinegar, he said, it is finished"** and also Revelation 21:6, **"And he said unto me, It is done. I am Alpha and Omega, the beginning and the end. I will give unto him that is athirst of the fountain of the water of life freely."**

Judith Moore

CHAPTER

1

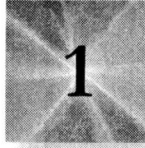

WHO IS THE BRIDE OF CHRIST?

The Bride of Christ

The question everyone is asking is, "Who really is the Bride of Christ?" It is much like when Jesus asked His disciples, "Who do you say that I am?" There are many diverse ideas and theories on this subject, and this book will not include them all.

Some say Israel is the Bride of Christ. They base their opinion on Isaiah 54:5, "For your Maker is your husband, the Lord of hosts is His name; and your Redeemer is the Holy One of Israel."

Others say the heavenly city, the New Jerusalem, is the Bride of Christ. They base their theory on the interpretation of Revelation 21:2-4.

Then I, John, saw the holy city, New Jerusalem, coming down out of heaven from God, prepared as a bride adorned for her husband. And I heard a loud voice from heaven saying, "Behold, the tabernacle of God is with men, and He will dwell with them, and they shall be His people. God

Himself will be with them and be their God. And God will wipe away every tear from their eyes; there shall be no more death, nor sorrow, nor crying. There shall be no more pain, for the former things have passed away."

The New Jerusalem was beautifully adorned *as* a Bride. John said that it is to be the eternal home of Christ's beloved Bride. But notice that it was a beautiful city **prepared as a Bride**; it was never called the **Bride**.

Supposedly the Bible teaches that perhaps the Church is the Bride of Christ. There are many in our churches that say, "there is a church within the Church," and that is the Bride of Christ. We find numerous ideas, but the Word of God will provide the answer in our study. It is important that we understand the difference between the Bride and the Body of Christ. Jesus didn't call us His bride for nothing! He wants us to get a picture of His love, His great delight, and His joyful delight in being with us.

The Secrets to New Insights and Preparations as The Bride

Following are some reasons for concluding that the Lord may come first for the Bride of Christ, and then the Body of Christ. The Body of Christ and the Bride of Christ are not the same. Godly men and women disagree on this issue. There is a strong tendency in our Adamic nature to want to be the speaker for God, "You shall be like gods." Nevertheless, "God has not given us a spirit of timidity but of power, love and a sound mind." There is very strong evidence indicating the Bride will be taken out of the Body of Christ. When Christians are asked about "Who is the Bride of Christ?" almost everyone answers, "The Church," or "The Body of Christ," meaning all saved people. However, nowhere in the Bible is the Church called the Bride of Christ. The Church is called His Body in Ephesians 1:22-23, but the Body and the Bride do not seem to be synonymous. The consequences of this are very significant and sobering.

Proverb 25:2 says a very important fact: "It is the glory of God to conceal a thing, but honor of kings is to search out a matter."

God's glory is concealed through His Word, but the believer as a king or priest should search it out. One of the richest veins of gold and silver in the Bible is in the Bride of Christ. It is a mine that is rarely dug into and much priceless metal and even valuable jewels are to be found there. Gold and silver are generally not found on the surface, but are found in deep mines. There are many jewels and treasures in the Word of God, but we must have a deeper relationship with the Lord in order to find them.

> Call unto me, and I will answer thee, and shew thee great and mighty things, which thou knowest not (Jeremiah 33:3).

We need to ask the Holy Spirit to show us the depths of His Word. The Scripture says in Acts 17:10 that the believers that lived in Berea did search the Scriptures daily.

> And the brethren immediately sent away Paul and Silas by night unto Berea: who coming thither went into the synagogue of the Jews. These were more noble than those in Thessalonica, in that they received the word with all readiness of mind, and searched the Scriptures daily, whether those things were so (Acts 17:10-11).

We must desire to search the Scriptures daily as we prepare to be His Bride. As we study the Scriptures, we should be like the Bereans and seek diligently with an open heart and mind in order to be a part of "The Glorious Bride who has prepared!" (The bride is responsible for making herself ready. Never will you find an example of a groom preparing the bride for the wedding. That is her responsibility and it is for each one of us as well.)

> Let us rejoice and be glad and give him glory! For the wedding of the Lamb has come, and his bride has made

herself ready. And it was given to her to clothe herself in fine linen, bright and clean; for the fine linen is the righteous acts of the saints (Revelation 19:7-8).

We must ask the questions: "Is the Bride of Christ literal or symbolic? Who or what is the Bride of Christ?" Many are confused about this identity that has come down from generation to generation. It will surprise some of you to know that this exact wording "the Bride of Christ," is not found in the Bible. This does not diminish the fact that it can be experienced and understood only by those who desire a deeper, intimate relationship with God. Intimacy with the Lord is very essential in being the Bride of Christ.

> *Intimacy with the Lord is very essential in being the Bride of Christ*

Let us look at the parallels of the marriage covenant and the Bride of Christ. At Mount Sinai, God proposed to the Israelites and entered into a covenant with them. This covenant was a marriage contract, which was sealed with the sprinkling of blood. Therefore, each marriage between a man and a woman should be sealed with blood through the consummation of the marriage as a witness and testimony of the covenant God makes with us. In Jeremiah 31:31, God declares His covenant as a marriage contract at Mount Sinai.

Behold, the days come, saith the LORD, that I will make a new covenant with the house of Israel, and with the house of Judah (Jeremiah 31:31).

It would benefit us to look at the church in Corinth, as Paul writes and exhorts them to hold fast to the simplicity of Christ, lest they are deceived and led astray by Satan from their devotion to Jesus. Paul was reminding them that he had, firsthand, delivered a message from Jesus containing His marriage proposal to them saying:

> For I am jealous over you with godly jealousy: for I have espoused you to one husband, that I may present you as a chaste virgin to Christ (2 Corinthians 11:2).

The message Paul preached was a marriage proposal of Christ to them. They were likely known as the Bride of Christ even though it does not specifically say that. This is true to all who partake of the cup and the bread, or communion, in that God is jealous over us with His love.

We should take a brief look at the ordinance of communion, which so many of us misunderstand and consequently undervalue the meaning of it. Most of us are familiar with the account of the Last Supper as we commonly call it, but which was in fact a traditional celebration of the Jewish Passover feast.

The gospel of Luke records these events.

> And when the hour was come, he sat down, and the twelve apostles with him. And he said unto them, "With desire I have desired to eat this Passover with you before I suffer: For I say unto you, I will not any more eat thereof, until it be fulfilled in the kingdom of God." And he took the cup, and gave thanks, and said, "Take this, and divide it among yourselves: For I say unto you, I will not drink of the fruit of the vine, until the kingdom of God shall come." And he took bread, and gave thanks, and brake it, and gave unto them, saying, "This is my body which is given for you: this do in remembrance of me." Likewise also the cup after supper, saying, "This cup is the new testament in my blood, which is shed for you" (Luke 22:14-20).

When we understand that Jesus was in effect betrothing to Himself a Bride at that first celebration of communion, we also begin to understand the deep covenant symbolized by the bread and wine. The celebration of communion is the celebration of intimacy with our spiritual Bridegroom. Each time we partake of the bread and wine we are accepting His proposal and pledging our faithfulness to Him. God takes covenant seriously; so should we.

It was not very much longer after that intimate Passover meal, that the Church was born as the blood and water gushed from the side of Christ, the last Adam. Just as the very first bride, Eve, had been brought forth from the side of the first Adam (see John 19:34).

Why was there another covenant made? Because the first covenant was of the letter and the letter kills; but the new covenant is of the Spirit and the Spirit gives life (see 2 Corinthians 3:6). This new covenant is another marriage contract that will not be broken. It was sealed with the shed blood of Jesus Christ on Calvary! Before Jesus was crucified, He gathered His apostles during His last Passover meal. It is important that we know about covenant and its significance in our relationship with the Lord.

> *The celebration of communion is the celebration of intimacy with our spiritual Bridegroom*

And he took the cup, and gave thanks, and gave it to them, saying, "Drink ye all of it; For this is my blood of the new testament, which is shed for many for the remission of sins. But I say unto you, I will not drink henceforth of this fruit of the vine, until that day when I drink it new with you in my Father's kingdom" (Matthew 26:27-29).

There are several key points to what Jesus said in this passage. First, we must understand Jewish wedding customs to grasp fully what Jesus was saying, and this will be explained further in chapter 6, "The Preparation Time is Now." When a Jewish man proposed marriage to a Jewish woman, he would give her a contract called a Ketubah. In the contract were all the promises to his future bride. It also stated the price he would pay to obtain her. If she agreed, the bridegroom would hand her a cup of wine. If she drank from the cup the marriage was sealed and they became legally married. He would then say to her, "I will not drink of this cup until we are re-united." This was said because they would separate for at least a year as he prepared a place for them. Another reason he would not drink of the cup again was because if he did, he would be proposing to someone else! No wonder Jesus said, "drink from it, all of you," because their acceptance of the cup meant they would be legally married.

He also said, "This is my blood of the covenant, which is poured out for many for the forgiveness of sins." In this statement Jesus was laying out the price He would pay to obtain His Bride. The wages of sin is death, and He paid this on our behalf (see Romans 6:23). He could pay this because He, Himself, was without sin (see Hebrews 4:15). Have you partaken of His cup that He offers each one of us? If you have, did you realize you have already accepted marriage to Jesus and He is your heavenly Bridegroom? Does this challenge you to be fully committed and to be faithful only to Him? It should, knowing that God has called you to now have an intimate relationship with Him. You therefore, should seek to know the depth of this relationship so you may have the following Scripture as reality in your life: "And to know the love of Christ, which passeth knowledge, that ye might be filled with all the fullness of God" (Ephesians 3:19)

Does communion have a different meaning now that you are betrothed to the Lord and have accepted Him as your Bridegroom?

The Lord Jesus Christ will soon return for His Bride. This will be the Bride that has been prepared. The awareness in the mind of much of the Church is that this Bride will consist of all believers. It is believed by many that the Bride will include the entire Body of Christ. Is this an accurate perception?

One does not have to look any further than the opening chapters of Genesis to begin to discern the truth of who the Bride is and where she will come from – God. In the first chapter of the Bible, we are told that God created man, fashioning him after His own image. God declared that it was not good that this first man (Adam) should remain alone, so a suitable helper was sought for him. This helper was to become the very first bride, and she would be a model, or type, of a latter bride who would come forth. This latter bride would be the Bride of Christ. The Bible begins with a marriage of the first Adam and ends with the last Adam (Jesus) in the Marriage Supper of the Lamb.

God ordained and established marriage and its divine sanctity in Genesis specifically when He brought Adam and Eve together to become one flesh in the marriage covenant (See Genesis 2:21-24). Adam is a type of Christ here (See Romans 5:14). God had caused a deep sleep to fall upon Adam. Sleep is sometimes synonymous with death (See Ephesians 5:14). The deep sleep that God caused to fall upon Adam is a picture of the crucifixion and death of Jesus. God brought a deep sleep upon Adam so that He could take a rib from the side of his flesh, which required the shedding of blood. This is a picture of Christ whose flesh was pierced in the side, shedding His own blood when He hung on the cross. From the rib of Adam, God created Eve. By the death of Jesus and our faith in Him, we become wedded to Him and thus, we become the Bride of Christ. By accepting, trusting, and believing in Jesus, we become one with Him, and we will know Him in an intimate way.

The Bride of Christ is to be "bone of His bone and flesh of His flesh." The Body is to be an extension of the Head. We are called to communicate to others, in these last days, the fullness of the Lord's ministry to bring in the harvest of the ages through many members in the body. The Lord is depicted as a lamb slain, having seven horns and seven eyes, which are the seven Spirits of God. The following Scripture points this out:

> And I looked, and behold, in the midst of the throne and of the four living creatures, and in the midst of the elders, stood a Lamb as though it had been slain, having seven horns and seven eyes, which are the seven Spirits of God sent out into all the earth (Revelation 5:6).

Wisdom and Revelation

It is important to understand wisdom and revelation, and see the significance of counsel, might, knowledge, and reverential awe. These are some of the facets that deserve our attention, if we are the Bride of Christ. We will see the brilliance of these facets in the light of the Lord; much like a diamond needs light to bring out its brilliance. The Lord will enlighten these facets in order for us to radiate His love.

For the release of the mantle of wisdom and understanding, we must pray and ask for it, as the apostle Paul taught in Ephesians 1:17-19. Equipping and instruction will result, helping us to appropriately understand the Biblical offices and administration. We must earnestly desire these mantles and pray for the maturity, character, and grace to be endowed with them.

There are many facets in a diamond. Those facets reflect light and make the jewel more brilliant. We will see that the advantages of being equipped are tremendous, upon the examination of the following four facets. :

- The eyes of our hearts are enlightened.

- Insight and wisdom to know what is the hope of His calling.

- Know the riches or wealth of the glory of His inheritance in the saints.

- Know the surpassing greatness of His power toward us who believe.

The spirit of wisdom is the supernatural ability of God that comes upon our spirits to comprehend and apprehend Jesus as He is, and receive that spiritual understanding and knowledge of God's Word that enables us to know what to do, when to do it and how to do it in every situation. It also reveals God's manifold and unsearchable wisdom and secrets that are affecting His plans and purposes for our Christian life. It definitely means a deeper intimacy into the things of God for each one of us. Ask yourself these questions: When people look at you, do they really see the characteristics of Christ? Do they hear godly wisdom in what you share from your mouth? Can they see godly love in your actions and reactions? And, is godly power visible in your life?

God doesn't want us to just have the revelation of Christ; He wants us to be a reproduction of Christ. Roman 8:29 validates this: "For whom he did foreknow, he also did predestinate to be conformed to the image of his Son, that he might be the firstborn among many brethren." We must be informed, so He can transform us and together we will be conformed into His image in the presence of the King.

Spirit of Understanding

The spirit of revelation and/or understanding is a comprehension and responsiveness to the things of God, providing understanding and giving insight. Wisdom and understanding mean the insight into the true nature of things with the ability to discern the mode of action with a view to their results. It is the ability to not only know the things of God, but also to know the application of them in our lives daily.

A revelation is the unveiling of the comprehension imparted into our spirits from the Holy Spirit and transmitted into our minds. It is the voice of God speaking to our spirits and informing our minds of that which God is going to do. It is the unfolding of hidden secrets to us by the Holy Spirit and the revealing of mysteries and insight into the future. We must unveil what the Lord has revealed to us in these last days so we can share these insights with others in the Body of Christ and He will be glorified.

If we are to function as the Bride of Christ and be the "light" of the world, we must possess qualities consistent with the Bridegroom. We must not only be consistent in our walk with the Lord, but we must also be constant in it as well. The children of Light will allow Christ to be fully manifested in us and He will be seen through our lives. Jesus said we would be "the light of the world" which means when all around us is dark; we will show the world how to come out of the darkness and into His marvelous light. These two verses confirm this:

> Ye are the light of the world. A city that is set on a hill cannot be hid (Matthew 5:14).

> Who hath delivered us from the power of darkness, and hath translated us into the kingdom of his dear Son (Colossians 1:13).

Our Directive

Though the Western church may look like a valley of dry bones as it is described in Ezekiel, I believe the Lord sees the Church prophetically as an exceedingly great army. We are convinced that our nation and the Western church have an incredible destiny yet to be fulfilled, as leaders among nations, to introduce the Bride of Christ universally. When people are given a glimpse of their individual role in that destiny, it transforms them and sets them on the course to repentance and the impartation of the Christ-like nature. Are you ready to be a part of that fulfillment and realize the destiny you have because of the Body and Bride of Christ?

They see the cause of God and are forever changed and have the joy of their salvation restored. We are seeing that happen at this present time in history. Strongholds of hopelessness, despair, depression, and other oppressive mind-sets will be overcome when God's life is breathed into this army and it begins to function as the Bride of the Bridegroom. We will very likely see the Bride of Christ arrayed in her wedding garment and in combat boots in the coming days ahead.

> *We must not only be consistent in our walk with the Lord, but we must also be constant in it as well*

We know that the Scripture tells us Jesus was filled with the power of the Holy Spirit. When Jesus came to His hometown, He went to the synagogue according to His custom. The news of His teaching, preaching, and healing ministry had already reached Nazareth. He was bestowed with the honor of reading the Scripture in the synagogue and of commenting upon it. The scroll of the prophet Isaiah was handed to Him and He began to read in Isaiah 61.

> The Spirit of the Lord is upon me because he has anointed me to bring good news to the poor. He has sent me to proclaim release to the captives and recovery of sight to the blind, to let the oppressed go free, to proclaim the year of the Lord's favor (Isaiah 61:1).

Jesus announced that this Scripture from God through Isaiah was, at that moment of time, being fulfilled by Him. When the folks of Nazareth heard these words quoted by Jesus, they thought Jesus was offering to be the kind of political Messiah that was popularly envisioned. They hoped He would throw off the yoke of Roman oppression. They swiftly turned on Him when Jesus made it plain that He was speaking of another kind of oppression – one that was spiritual in nature. They were in bondage to sin, not just to Roman rule, and the freedom that Jesus offered involved God's liberating forgiveness, not a political uprising. When Jesus said, "Today this Scripture has been fulfilled in your hearing," it was, indeed, an extreme and radical statement, but not in the way in which people understood it.

Paul, too, sought to bring revolutionary concepts to the church in Corinth. He has just finished explaining about spiritual gifts, and how each person has an allotted gift to be used in order to make distinctions among themselves.

> For just as the body is one and has many members, and all the members of the body, though many, are one body, so it is with Christ. For in the one Spirit we were all baptized into one body – Jews or Greeks, slaves or free – and we were all made to drink of one Spirit (1 Corinthians 12:13).

Paul is addressing his concerns related to the desires of the members of the church at Corinth to boast of their spiritual superiority. Such boasting was leading to division and unrest in the church and it would probably have the same effect in our churches today. Certain members of the church were quarreling and forming competitive circles, each of which claimed to be more spiritual than the next. Paul desperately needed a new image to get his message across and he chose this wonderful image of the body. Think about it for a moment. This may have caused the first division in the Church.

The human body has hundreds of parts. Not one, or two or three of them, taken alone or together, would amount too much of anything. Taken all together, they join to form one of God's most awesome creations. The New Testament describes the image of the Church in this way: In 1 Corinthians 3, the Church is compared to a field and to a building. In Ephesians 5, the Church is compared to a Bride. In each of these comparisons, the Church is "like" this, or "like" that. But then, in this passage from Corinthians, Paul says: "The Church is the Body of Christ." He doesn't say "like" the Body of Christ. He says we "ARE" the Body of Christ. With this image, Paul is giving us a new blueprint for the Church, a prescription for building a healthy Body of Christ.

The first characteristic of a healthy Body of Christ, Paul tells us, is unity - all the parts working together for one purpose. In 1 Corinthians 12:12 it says, "For just as the body is one and has many members, and all the members of the body, though many, are one body, so it is with Christ." Throughout the New Testament we can find constant warnings against letting ourselves to be distracted by arguments and dissension. It is as if the apostles are saying, "Come on, can't we all just get along? Is what you're arguing about going to bring people to Christ?" The apostles had only one mind, the mind of Christ, to guide everything they did.

They had only one purpose in life - to spread the good news of Christ. When you identify your greatest priority in life, it is not unusual for the little details to fall by the wayside. They're simply not important anymore. Until the Church has one mind and one purpose, we will continue to get distracted by such trivial matters. The best way for us to destroy the image and Body of Christ is to argue with each other. Satan loves for us to be at odds with our fellow brothers and sisters in the Lord. He gets us to fight each other and then he doesn't have to be the one that gets the blame for the division within the Body of Christ.

There is an interesting story by Pat Williams about Chad Sheron, a doctor and former basketball player at Vanderbilt University, who combined his knowledge of teamwork and medicine to describe how a body is supposed to work in unity. He was a medical student and he observed that the various cells of the human body – muscle cells, blood cells, organ cells, bone cells, and all the other cells – all are designed to work together to enhance the health and life of the entire body. But occasionally, a cell can begin growing and functioning out of sync with the other cells. It begins growing for its own purposes and no longer follows the same blueprint as the other cells. This type of cell is called a "mutagen," and mutagens are the cells that create a cancer in the body. As Chad says, "Just as mutagens cause cancer in the human body, people who behave like mutagens can have a cancerous effect on a team."[1] (Or on a church!)

If that principle is true for a sports team, it's very true for a church team or the Body of Christ. All the individual members must work together to enhance the health and life of the entire body. People who behave only for their own sake and not for the good of the Body of Christ have a cancerous effect on Christ's Church—they pull from and drain its resources. As Christians are in tune, or wanting to be in tune, with the Holy Spirit's agenda, we'll want to pull in the same direction of the Spirit – not away from – so we will seek unity, not fragmentation or division. If we, as the Body of Christ, would realize that we share one mind and one purpose, if nothing else in life mattered to us as much as sharing the good news of Jesus, we could transform our whole world.

How sad it is then, to watch churches and denominations tearing themselves apart, increasing rather than decreasing divisions, as they draw lines to exclude certain categories of people, or worse yet, certain categories of Christians, from their worship or from their pulpits. Subtraction and division have always been the devil's tools. Yet, addition and multiplication are the tools of the Body of Christ. Some denominations have sought to bar women from ordination, and almost every denomination is drawing lines, either in sand or in

---

1 Williams, Pat, *The Magic of Teamwork* (Nashville: Thomas Nelson Publishers, 1997)

concrete, about their rights within the Body. They need to go back and reread this part of Paul's message. Paul tells us that the second characteristic of a healthy Body of Christ is equality. A healthy Body of Christ values all members equally.

> Nay, much more those members of the body, which seem to be more feeble, are necessary: And those members of the body, which we think to be less honourable, upon these we bestow more abundant honour; and our uncomely parts have more abundant comeliness. For our comely parts have no need: but God hath tempered the body together, having given more abundant honour to that part which lacked: That there should be no schism in the body; but that the members should have the same care one for another (1 Corinthians 12:22-25).

My significance to the Church is no greater than any other member. Every last one of us, from the youngest to the oldest, the richest to the poorest, is equally valuable and important. We must realize that our goal is to complete each other and not to compete with each other. We all are important to carry out the work of the Lord. Let each one of us start to do what we can to complete one another. We will have a more complete picture as to the Body of Christ and make a more beautiful Bride of Christ.

Check out the value system of Jesus. He loved the outcast, the poor, the disabled, the unclean, the sinner. Why? It is because you have to value each of these simply because of whose you are. You belong to the Lord and His family. Makes us all sit up and take notice, doesn't it? At your job, you may feel like just another number on a time card. In your other relationships you may feel like you are not being heard and recognized and feel like a nobody. But in the Church, you are of infinite value and you are significant to the Body of Christ. You have skills, abilities, and life experiences that other people need. You are vitally important to the Body of Christ.

You do things that only you can do; and others also have a function as well. Again, we must learn the fact that we are completing each other, and not competing with each other.

The final characteristic of a healthy Body of Christ, mentioned by Paul, is empathy. We are called to share another's joys and sorrows. As 1 Corinthians 12: 26 says, "If one part suffers, every part suffers with it; if one part is honored, every part rejoices with it." We were not meant to bear our burdens alone. The Body of Christ was meant to suffer with those who suffer and rejoice with those who rejoice. That is one of the reasons why we share joys and concerns during our prayer time each week and why we invite many to accept the responsibility to pray for those whose needs are lifted up to the Lord.

A pastor once told this story about visiting Lester, an elderly man suffering from cancer. Often, Lester was in such pain that he would just lie on the bed and moan softly, "Oh me. Oh me." One day, the pastor happened by when Lester's son was visiting. He was appalled to see the son lean down close to his father and repeat "Oh me. Oh me," as if he were mocking the older gentleman.

The son, noting the pastor's dismay, quickly explained. Before coming to the hospital, Lester had lived with his son, daughter-in-law, and his two-year-old grandson, Wesley. Little Wesley loved to "help" his grandfather. He would come alongside him, grab the bottom of his walking cane, and walk with Lester around the house. Wesley would also demonstrate his friendship by echoing his grandfather's moans, "Oh me. Oh me." In his own way, little Wesley was trying to share his grandfather's pain. That's what a healthy Body of Christ does: we walk alongside one another and share another's pain.

I'm not trying to make anybody feel guilty, but try to take a moment out of your busy schedule and look at the people that are around you. Look you at their lives for a moment. Whether you know it or not, there are people on all sides of you, whose hearts are breaking or who are engaged in some kind of personal struggle: people who are confused, angry, lost, scared, broken in spirit. Some have suffered a personal loss, others struggle with job and career choices, while still others just need a friend to listen. There is someone that needs you. You need them. That's what the Church is all about. We don't have to go through life alone. We need to encourage someone else in his or her walk with the Lord now, and not wait till tomorrow. It may be too late tomorrow. Do it today.

It is interesting to talk about the Body from the reference in 1 Corinthians 12:1-31. What follows is an elaborate illustration in which Paul likens the Church to a human body with each part playing its own vital role. His purpose is clearly to affirm the importance of the unity of the Church and the place of each member in the body. In particular, he reminds those who are glorying in the gifts that God has given them and looking on those whose gifts are not so impressive, that in the Body of Christ, as in a human body, every member is important and its proper function depends upon every member serving the interests of the whole body.

> *The Body of Christ is to complete each other and not to compete with each other*

In 1 Corinthians 12:13 we see that the diversity in the Body of Christ is by God's own design; and by verse 21 it is clearly reflecting the fact that some in the Corinthian church seemed to feel that they did not need the others, that their superior rank – perhaps socially, but certainly in respect to the spiritual gifts they had been given – rendered them self-sufficient.

Pride takes on many forms. Sin usually makes every human a lover of himself or herself, but takes many different forms. People can express the pride and self-love raging in their hearts by looking down on others or by anxiously looking up to be sure that no one is looking down at them. Both of those expressions of pride could be found in the church of Corinth. There were those full of concern that the churches and their leaders seem as impressive as those of the world.

You find, of course, all of these same habits of mind and conditions of heart in the Church today. Pride lurks everywhere, around every corner; it sits on the edge of many of the words we speak, and it motivates our thoughts and attitudes even when we are unaware of it. We are always looking at others, thinking about others and comparing ourselves to others from the vantage point of our own self-worship.

Any minister will tell you that when the Lord helps him to preach a powerful sermon and God's people are stirred by it, it is almost impossible for him not to bask in the glory of their appreciation and of the sermon's power, even though he knows full well it was God who gave him that sermon and God who made it powerful. Jean Massillon, the great French preacher, told about an incident after a service in which he had preached one of his characteristically eloquent and powerful sermons. A woman lavished praise on him. He promptly replied, "Madam, the devil has already said that to me and much more eloquently than you."[2]

It is interesting that in the other passage in which Paul discusses the gifts that the Holy Spirit distributes throughout the Church, in Romans 12:3-5, he makes the same point.

> For I say, through the grace given unto me, to every man that is among you, not to think of himself more highly than he ought to think; but to think soberly, according as God hath dealt to every man the measure of faith. For as we have many members in one body, and all members have not the same office: So we, being many, are one body in Christ, and every one members one of another (Romans 12:3-5).

2 *The Columbia Encyclopedia*, Sixth Edition 2008, s.v. "Jean Baptiste Massillon," from Encyclopedia.com (April 29, 2009)

Paul makes a direct attack on that pride. He lays the ax to its root in several ways. His purpose is not to compliment them for their gifts. We all have been guilty of pride because you either think well of yourself because of the gifts God has given you or you envy those who have the gifts you do not have. You either think more highly of yourself than you ought to think or resent the perceived superiority of others around you.

First, Paul says, those things that distinguish you, or what make others notice you that you are so easily tempted to pride yourself on, are all God's gifts to you. These spiritual gifts are just that – gifts. Everything else that is worthy and admirable in your life is God's gift to you. As Paul said to them earlier in this same letter, "What do you have that you did not receive?" You didn't earn these things, any more than you earned your appearance or some talent that you have. You didn't deserve these things and you certainly cannot take credit for them.

In other words, you have these gifts because God saw fit to give them to you. He might just as well have given them to someone else. When you think and act as if these gifts – whether tongues and interpretation in the days of the Corinthian church, or teaching, helping, serving, giving, exercising leadership, and so on that are listed here and elsewhere in the New Testament – you are forgetting yourself and you are forgetting what these things are: a present God gave you. When you are tempted to think highly of yourself, just remember what other believers will think of you if they know that you are taking personal credit for the gifts that God has so kindly given to you in spite of your sinfulness.

Second, your gifts are but a small part of the gifts of Christ's Body. The Church requires the entire range of the Holy Spirit's gifts and you have but one or two of them. Others have been given gifts that are likewise critical to the church's life. The pituitary gland is very small, but have you ever seen the woe it causes in a human life when it does not work properly? And now we understand that even genes, tiny as they are, control great things in the human body. You are not enough trying to do it on your own; your gifts depend upon the presence of the gifts of others as well. We tend to think that this is not so, that we are somehow uniquely indispensable, but that is just another lie that our pride is always whispering to our hearts.

It is to make this point that Paul uses his wonderful illustration of the body and its various members. Each depends on the other. It is really quite funny to think about it. The eye says to the hand, "I don't need you." And the hand says in return, "Oh no? Well, here's looking at you," and sticks a finger in the eye. Or the head says to the feet, "Take a walk!" And the feet do, right into the pool until the head is underwater and drowning. It is, Paul says, as absurd as that, when Christians act like they are self-sufficient and don't need each other. The Spirit's distribution of His gifts (this is Paul's point) proves that everyone else is important too. You are not required to think that everyone else is better, or more important than you are – that is false humility – but you are required to think that everyone else is as important as you are!

Third, Paul says, it isn't the possession of the gift but the use of it that is the measure of a Christian man or woman. This is the point that Paul brings love into the argument, with 1 Corinthians chapter 13, the famous "Love Chapter."

> If I speak with the tongues of men and of angels, but have not love, I am only a resounding gong or a clanging cymbal (v.1).

You have gifts and can impress everyone around you with your importance, but if you are not using God's gifts to serve others in Christ's name or for His body, if you are more concerned with applause than with love for God and man, then your gifts only increase your guilt and aggravate your sin. God and the Holy Spirit gave you His gifts – not for your sake, but for the sake of others!

Usually when people tell me what they think their spiritual gift is, it is one of the prominent gifts, and is usually teaching. Teaching, after all, places us in front of other people, it serves to get us attention, if we do it well people will admire us and even come to depend upon us. But, characteristically, the Bible says that teaching is a sacred trust. It's for the purpose of building up God's people not the teacher, and that your teaching will be measured in the great day not by how much you were admired for it or how much you may have enjoyed the limelight, but rather by how well you served the saints. "Let few be teachers," we are warned, "for they will be judged more strictly." This comes from James 3:1.

Naturally we tend to think that the more gifted we are, the more fortunate. The Bible doesn't say that. It says, the more gifted we are, the more responsible and accountable we are to use them properly. Every gift is a stewardship for the exercise of which we will have to give an account. If we could just see the day of judgment in our mind's eye and ourselves going up to the great white throne, we would care much less about what gifts the Holy Spirit may have seen fit to give us, and much, much more about the faithful and loving exercise of our simple duties every day.

> *The more gifted we are, the more responsible and accountable we are to use those gifts properly*

People often wonder how to discover their gifts. The Bible doesn't tell you to go to a seminar to find out. Seminars don't seem to care much what your gift is in the Body of Christ. The Lord cares much more that you love your brothers and sisters. After all, each spiritual gift is also, in some way, an ordinary duty that we need to perform. Every Christian has teaching to do, as a parent, as a friend, as a witness. Every Christian has serving and giving to do and so on. Do you do all of those things with a heart of love for God? Do you find that others see that you do certain things particularly well? Those are the gifts of the Spirit that God has given you.

Paul's simple but profound counsel to us is so fundamental. Some of you are better at one thing more than others. Others of you are gifted in this way or another way. You may be wondering – do I even have a gift? The important fact is that the Lord's chief concern is that you love one another and care for each other in that spirit of humility, and that you are a suitable servant to sinners saved by grace. The measure of your life is not your gift – but your love. Whether you are a hand, an eye, or the head, the Lord will measure your life by how well - and how humbly through love - you have served the feet, elbows, and knees of the Body of Christ. It is all about our donation of our gift to others and not just the duration. We need to allow the love of the Lord to flow through us in all we do and for His glory.

We may have impressive gifts or unimpressive gifts. That is the Spirit's business and His doing. But we can all love and we can all live our lives for the sake of this truth: "What do you give to the Body of Christ that brings glory and honor to Him?" There are lots of gifted people in the Church and in the world. There are many known and celebrated for their gift, yet there are fewer who are known for their humility and for their love. Let us aspire to be found in that smaller group for Jesus' sake.

There are many gifts, one Spirit – many members, one Body. We are the Body of Christ, empowered by the Holy Spirit to live and to work in unity with each other. "We were all baptized into one body – Jews, Greek, slaves or free – and all were made to drink of one Spirit." One Spirit baptizes us into the one Body, the Church.

Sharing the common cup reinforces our unity in the one Body. However, this union must be expressed not only sacramental, in our relationship with God, but also sacrificially, in our relationship with one another.

We are all linked together and are stronger because of relationship with each other. This linking together makes a strong chain, but we are only as strong as our weakest link. We need to depend on each other for strength. We are the Body of Christ. We are one. We are equal and inter-dependent, and we are called to love and to care for each other. If one suffers, let us suffer together. If one rejoices, let us rejoice together. And let us use the gifts of the Spirit, which God has given us to build up the Body of Christ. In conclusion, we will learn to complete each other and not to compete with one another in the Body of Christ. Amen!

CHAPTER

2

THE BRIDAL COMPANY IN EVE AND ESTHER

The Bride of Christ is a Bride that is chosen, prepared, arrayed, and made ready for this role – fitted to the prescribed and the consequent glory that will be experienced. Those who are the Bride of Christ should be cognizant of this great future. They should be properly and submissively conducting themselves as befits the Bride. Imagine the consummation of this phenomenal event – when Christ will take unto Himself His Bride whom He has chosen, purchased, ransomed, and prepared for this time.

Before time as we know it, God set out to make a Bride for Himself. God knew this would not be an easy task, but it was phenomenal how that God created man and woman. It was one thing to make the animals male and female, but it was another thing to make a Bride for Himself. Suppose there was a council in the Godhead meeting and this is what was decided:

And God said, "Let us make man in our image, after our likeness: and let them have dominion over the fish of the sea, and over the fowl of the air, and over the cattle, and over all the earth, and over every creeping thing that creeps upon the earth" (Genesis 1:26).

Did you know that God could have made man in the image of the angels or some animal, but instead He did something altogether very different? He made man in His own image and resemblance, according to the Scripture. God wanted Adam to have a mate who could relate to him and have fellowship with him on his level. God wanted someone for Adam who would love him as he loved, and not obey him because she had to, but to obey out of her love relationship with him. He also wanted a ruling counterpart, a queen or woman, who could rule with him over God's creation.

The Bible is full of images in regard to brides. These images were given to provide understanding of the ultimate bride, which is the Bride of Christ. Both the Old and the New Testament describe how God through Christ, the Bridegroom, is in the process of marrying His Bride. They are the believers in Him, who will ultimately live and dwell with Him forever. The ones who are a part of the Bride of Christ now are the ones who will live not only ultimately with Him forever, but who live intimately with Him now.

God had given Adam the ability to commune with nature and animals as we see in Genesis 1:19 & 20, yet Adam still was not secure and complete. God was helping Adam to become aware of his need for more than communion with God and nature. Man was becoming aware of his need for oneness with a woman. There was something about union and unity in God's plan for man and woman. Until Adam saw this, maybe he could not be trusted with a woman. Today, men must see their need for intimacy with God first, and then their family. The man saw the need of a woman as far more important than sports, nature, business, and ministry; otherwise it was difficult for him to be completed with a woman.

God created a bride for the first Adam from a rib taken from Adam's body. In similar fashion, He is even now creating a Bride for the last Adam, Jesus Christ. Even as the first Adam was put to sleep and a rib was removed from his side in order to fashion for him a bride; likewise, the last Adam was put to sleep on the cross, a spear went between His ribs into His side, and the provision for His Bride — blood and water. We are told in Leviticus 17:11 that "the life of the flesh is in the blood." This Bride is not Christ's entire Body, even as Eve was not fashioned from Adam's entire body. The Bride of Christ will be fashioned from a remnant of Christ's Body or from the Church. God made the Bride from a unique plan.

God ordained and established marriage and its divine sacredness in Genesis. He brought Adam and Eve together to become one flesh (See Genesis 2:21-24). God caused a deep sleep to fall upon Adam. He would take a rib from the side of his flesh, and it was from that rib of Adam that God made Eve.

For this cause shall a man leave his father and mother, and shall be joined unto his wife, and they two shall be one flesh (Ephesians 5:31).

Let's observe Old Testament references regarding the subject of the Bride. It is important to reiterate that the Bible is full of images of brides. Biblical pictures of the Bride were given to provide understanding of the ultimate bride, which is the Bride of Christ. It is in the book of Esther that we read of a bride that was prepared for a king. Even so, the Bride of Christ is being prepared for her King. Esther is a type of the church within the Church. She represents the Bride of Christ, who is being prepared to come into the presence of the King of Kings. Esther is the bride who was chosen to live in a love relationship with the king without any regard required to qualify her for that relationship.

This book of Esther is not just an ordinary story. It is a beautiful example of how one unsuspecting woman was chosen by God "for such a time as this" to be in the right place at the right time. It's not that she was better than anyone else, she was obedient and sacrificed her self-will in order to come to the king. Esther is a true representation of being the Bride of Christ, or some would say even the Church. This book will show that there is a big difference between these two – the Church and the Bride. This story in Esther will reveal how she prepared herself, and how it will have application for us today. Like Esther, our goal is to be in the presence of the King, in the throne room, with His scepter extended in favor toward us.

> *Like Esther, our goal is to be in the presence of the King, in the throne room, with His scepter extended in favor toward us*

Queen Esther was called for a time and a purpose, but she made the choice to yield to this calling; to go through the cleansing, the preparation, the purifying, and even the beautifying to come before the king. She could have chosen to run in the opposite direction, but her heart was full of the love of God for His people. She desired to see them free above the love of her own life. She loved not her life unto death if need be. "If He slay me, yet will I trust Him" must be the cry of your heart.

We find in the book of Esther, that King Xerxes had many virgins from which to choose, but only one found favor with him and that was Esther. Esther was the highly favored one among all the women and was set apart to be the queen. Therefore, Esther had favor not only with God, but also with man.

The king loved Esther above all the other women, and she obtained grace and favor in his sight more than all the virgins; that he set the royal crown upon her head, and made her queen (Esther 2:17).

44

The Biblical character, Mordecai, was a type of the Holy Spirit who led Esther and encouraged and even challenged her. Every day that she was in the 12-month period of preparation, Mordecai inquired at the palace gates to see how Esther was progressing. Esther was an orphan and she would never have made it without Mordecai. Neither will we, unless we have a very intimate relationship with our Lord, and we will need the Holy Spirit that will encourage us in our preparation time. Just as it took Esther twelve months to prepare to be the queen, we must realize in this day and time we are approaching the midnight hour, and we too should be in preparation to meet our King of Kings. The Holy Spirit is relating to many in Christian groups about the hour in which we are living – the end times.

In the third year of the reign of Xerxes, he gave a banquet and "displayed the riches of his royal glory and the splendor of his great majesty for many days..." (Esther 1:4). On the seventh day of this great banquet, he commanded his eunuchs to bring his wife Vashti into the banquet. It is vital to see how the others perceived Vashti, and how this shows that she was a beautiful woman.

> On the seventh day, when the heart of the king was merry with wine, he commanded Mehuman, Biztha, Harbona, Bigtha, and Abagtha, Zethar, and Carcas, the seven chamberlains that served in the presence of Ahasuerus the king, to bring Queen Vashti before the king with her royal crown in order to display her beauty to the people and the princes, for she was beautiful (Esther 1:10-11).

King Ahasuerus is also known as Xerxes in this story. On the 7th day Xerxes summoned his queen to come before him, but because she did not revere him, as she should have, she refused to answer his summons. We can gain insight from the book of Esther that will benefit our preparation as a bride as well.

If it pleases the king, let a royal edict be issued by him and let it be written in the laws of Persia and Media so that it cannot be repealed, that Vashti should come no more into the presence of King Ahasuerus, and let the king give her royal position to another who is more worthy than she (Esther 1:19).

Due to her disobedience, Vashti was no longer permitted to enter the presence of the king. Much of the Body of Christ today also is failing in obedience to their King, and they will be excluded from the honor of entering into His presence as a Bride. The cost of obedience is nothing compared to the cost of disobedience.

Like Esther, our goal is to be in the presence of the King, in the throne room, and with His scepter of favor extended toward us. "Another who is more worthy" will be accorded this honor. For all those saints who have been falsely taught that salvation by faith affords them all of the honor of heaven and access to God's presence, as well as access to all of God's most holy things, this is a wake-up call. It is those who are worthy and have an intimate relationship with Him that will be granted such honor. Intimacy with the Lord will be a key factor in this relationship.

It does not say that Vashti was killed, or cast out; she was simply stripped of her honor. How terrible to be betrothed to the king, yet be denied access to his presence. It was shame, due to her foolishness, that followed her for the rest of her life. Queen Vashti must have encountered tremendous grief when her royal position was given to another. Yet, many in the Body of Christ today are failing in their obedience, and they will be excluded from the honor of entering into His presence into the bridal chamber. Shame and grief will be their portion as well. We are in a time in history when it is no longer "church as usual" and there is no time for foolishness. There is always a price to pay for our disobedience. This statement cannot be emphasized enough — the cost of obedience is nothing compared to the cost of disobedience.

Intimacy with God is of utmost importance. Our understanding of the kingdom of God takes a spectacular turn when we realize our first calling is to love and enjoy Jesus Christ. It is more than by fear or a sense of commitment; our obedience to Him must be fueled by our love and devotion for Him or it becomes reduced to dead works. It is passionate love, vibrant faith and boundless joy that call us as the Bride of Christ.

Much of the Body of Christ has been presented with a distorted view of God's desire for them. They have been taught to express faith in Jesus Christ to attain salvation only. Some of the Church knows that salvation is only the beginning of their relationship with the Lord and there is a lot in between before we get to the end as a Bride of Christ. Salvation releases us from the bondage of sin, so that we should forevermore become slaves to righteousness, as it is mentioned in Romans 6. We were formerly conforming to the ways of a fallen and sinful world,

> *The cost of obedience is nothing compared to the cost of disobedience*

but now we are to be conforming to the image of Christ (Romans 8:29). This conformation comes as a process, and salvation is the first step.

Many saints today, having confessed faith in Christ, are then assured by others that they can now continue to pursue personal happiness much as they did before salvation. They are even taught that God will be there to help them achieve the selfish longings of their hearts. The Lordship of Christ is often overlooked, or given very minimal attention. Such saints ultimately fall into the pattern of Queen Vashti. They love the honor of being wed to the King, but they see the King as existing only to meet their needs. Obedience is essentially foreign to them. They obey only when God's desire for them coincides with their own desire. When Jesus calls those who have been betrothed to Him to respond in obedience in this hour, many will refuse. Jesus will then respond as King Ahasuerus did in that He will restrict access from His presence to the disobedient ones. He will then search for another who is more worthy to be His Bride. This obedient Bride will be given honor and afforded access to His presence.

> *This obedient Bride will be given honor and afforded access to His presence*

We are told that after the anger of King Ahasuerus subsided, he remembered his queen but it was too late. He could not repeal the royal edict, so his advisers counseled him to have a new queen sought out. Beautiful virgins from all over his kingdom were gathered to his capital and placed under the care of Hegai, the eunuch in charge of the king's harem. Hegai was charged with the responsibility of preparing these chosen ones to meet the king. Esther was among those picked for consideration to become the bride of Ahasuerus. Once selected, these beautiful young virgins were not immediately ready to go into the king's chamber.

> For the days of their beautification were completed as follows: six months with oil of myrrh and six months with spices and the cosmetics for women (Esther 2:12).

It was only after the virgin went through a year of preparation that she was ready to be presented to the king. The first six months of this process were marked by the pronounced usage of oil of myrrh. Myrrh should be recognized by most as a spice that was used in preparing bodies for burial. After Christ's crucifixion we are told that His body was prepared for burial and myrrh is especially mentioned. It is significant in the description of this event found in the book of John that it repeatedly states that Christ's body was taken away and prepared.

> And after these things Joseph of Arimathea, being a disciple of Jesus, but a secret one, for fear of the Jews, asked Pilate that he might take away the body of Jesus; and Pilate granted permission. He came therefore, and took away His body. And Nicodemus came also, who had first come to Him by nigh bringing a mixture of myrrh and aloes, about a hundred pounds weight. And so they took the body of Jesus, and bound it in linen wrappings with the spices, as is the burial custom of the Jews (John 19:38-40).

Myrrh, for the virgin bridal applicants of the king, represented death as well. The one chosen to be the bride of the king was to live for the king's pleasure and in the king's palace. She was to respond to his summons and call with quick obedience. No longer was her life her own. Esther now belonged to another. Essentially, she was to die to her own life. Dying to self is always a painful process. The Scriptures tell those betrothed to Christ that they are no longer their own, "For you have been bought with a price" (1 Corinthians 6:20). Death is the first step of preparation that those who would become the Bride of Christ must go through. Salvation is not an end. It is a beginning of a new life. Our salvation was purchased with the blood of Jesus. The purchase price was exceedingly high, but it was paid. We are now no longer our own. We must die to our own desires, goals, and ambitions and be quick to obey.

Christ's life must become our life, His will our will, His desire our desire. This death process doesn't come all at once, or in a single moment of time. The flesh's desire to seek after self is firmly entrenched in our being. It takes considerable time just to identify all of the ways in which we have sought our own welfare. Some forms of selfishness are very subtle.

The Scriptures teach us that even our righteousness, which we deem to be good, will be as filthy rags in God's sight (see Isaiah 64:6). It is in this death process that obedience is learned and an end of personal initiative is brought forth. This time of preparation is designed to produce a suitable and compatible Bride for Christ. She must become like Him, conformed to His image. There are not any options in this process. We would like to have the end result without the process we have to go through to get it. There are no shortcuts or easy fixes for any of us.

Death to His own personal initiative and ambition were characteristics of Jesus. It was exemplified in His words at Gethsemane, "Nevertheless, not My will, but Thy will be done" (Luke 22:42). This was an attribute that Vashti lacked and it cost her that which was most precious to her. It is appropriate that this failure was the first thing addressed among those who would contend for the opportunity to replace Vashti. It will likewise be the foremost issue addressed among those who are called to be the Bride of Christ.

> *Christ's life must become our life, His will our will, His desire our desire*

In the story of King Ahasuerus' search for a suitable bride, we see some profound truths that are equally applicable to the Bride of Christ. The king's first bride was rejected due to a failure of obedience. A more worthy bride was then chosen to replace the one who had disqualified herself. Those called to be betrothed to Christ need to take this lesson to heart. As we will see in subsequent chapters, many are called, but few are chosen. Esther distinguished herself and was set apart by her obedience. She listened to the voice of the king's eunuch who was given charge over her, to prepare her, and found favor in the eyes of the king. Those four aspects are as follows:

1. There is a preparation time

Esther allowed herself to be prepared for the task. God's preparation time can sometimes be long and uneventful. Remember that Moses spent 40 years in the desert looking after sheep before coming to deliver and look after people, the Israelites. He had to learn how to lead sheep in order to lead the Israelites out of Egypt. Joseph was prepared for the palace by being placed in a pit by his brothers. He literally went from the pit to the palace and Moses went from the palace to the pit of tending sheep. God will divinely guide each of our steps and each of our stops. Many Bible characters received their training in and through a time of preparation. The refining of our character is very essential to God's plan for our life. God can not use a proud woman (or man). We all go through a preparation time and sometimes through a furnace of affliction in order to be in His will.

2. We need the favor of God

Esther found favor with the king and so did Mordecai. Even Jesus grew in favor with God and man (see Luke 2:52). When you live a life pleasing to God by obeying His will, you will find favor with Him. God will also give you favor with people as well.

3. God works in His own time and season

Esther also got her timing right. Maybe God has put it on your heart to do something for Him. We must wait for God's timing, because we serve an on-time God. Joseph was in jail until it was God's time for him to be released. God will move in His time when we remain faithful and alert to His leading. "My times are in thy hand" (Psalm 31:15a).

4. Your background does not hinder your future with God

Esther was an orphan. God still exalted her and used her. Her past did not determine her destiny. Some of Jesus' disciples were fishermen, one a tax collector, and one was a doctor. Your background does not determine what God can do with you, your faith does. We must not allow our past to block our future when we have a calling of God on our life.

Please re-read the book of Esther and see what else may be gleaned from this book. Even though God is never mentioned in that book of Esther, we see God's hand throughout it.

> So it came to pass, when the king's commandment and his decree was heard, and when many maidens were gathered together unto Shushan the citadel, to the custody of Hegai, that Esther was brought also unto the king's house, to the custody of Hegai, keeper of the women. And the maiden pleased him, and she obtained kindness of him; and he speedily gave her her beautifying ointments, with such things as belonged to her, and seven maidens, who were suitable to be given her, out of the king's house: and he moved her and her maidens unto the best place of the house of the women. Esther had not revealed her people nor her kindred: for Mordecai had charged her that she should not show it (Esther 2:8-10).

These verses represent how we too must learn to acknowledge and recognize the control of God over our lives in order to be anointed. Esther was literally anointed with special oils and perfumes to be purified, in order to be what God called her to be at that time in history. As followers of Jesus, we first soak in the glory of God or in His presence, just as Esther did in the oils and perfumes. In order for Esther to present herself to the king, she spent six months soaking in myrrh. The number 6 represents the flesh, and the myrrh was used in burial ceremonies. Esther had to die to self and even though it is painful, we must do the same – die daily. Then, she spent another six months soaking in the oil, which represents the Holy Spirit of God. This brings healing and completeness in her process of becoming queen. Esther had to be anointed so she could be appointed to fulfill her calling in God.

We are to be the Bride of Christ and it only makes sense that we prepare ourselves in the same technique as Esther. Once we have entered into the gates, it is our desire to go into the Holy of Holies. This is where we seek God's face, not just His hand. But in order to approach this place, we must be prepared to minister to God and not the other way around. We must remember our priorities at this point. This is the place where we no longer ask God what He can do for us, but what we can do for Him! Unless we become willing to make sacrifices in our own lives, we will always remain in the outer courts, and not much happens out there.

> *Your background does not determine what God can do with you, your faith does*

We want to be where the intimacy can take place without all the busyness. It is not business as usual in the Holy of Holies.

It was Esther's desire to attend to her king and ask, "What can I do for you?" She was not getting ready to make demands on him. In being a mature Christian, we know that it's not about us, it's ALL about Him and the role we both play in this sacred place. Once you have entered into the Holy of Holies, you don't feel the need to ask God for anything, because you know that He already knows all your needs and is prepared to give them to you. It will become our automatic response to give Him all the praise, honor and glory.

Another important aspect for Esther was her humility and how to respond to human responsibility.

So Esther was taken unto king Ahasuerus into his house royal in the tenth month, which is the month Tebeth, in the seventh year of his reign. And the king loved Esther above all the women, and she obtained grace and favor in his sight more than all the virgins; so that he set the royal crown upon her head, and made her queen instead of Vashti (Esther 2:16-17).

> *"Let us be glad and rejoice, and give honor to him: for the marriage of the Lamb is come, and his wife hath made herself ready"*

The king desired Esther just as God desires us today. She took the responsibility upon herself to be restored and she made herself ready for her king. There is a Scripture in Revelation 19:7 that says, "Let us be glad and rejoice, and give honor to him: for the marriage of the Lamb is come, and his wife hath made herself ready." If we are part of the Bride of Christ, are we making ourself ready for Him? This is the premise of how to make yourself ready for your Bridegroom.

Have the boldness to enter into the Holiest by the blood of Jesus. By a new and living way, which He has consecrated for us, through the veil, that is to say, His flesh. Let us draw near with a true heart in full assurance of faith, having our hearts sprinkled from an evil conscience, and our bodies washed with pure water (Hebrews 10:19-22 AMP.).

A glorious Church, and not just one that is anointed, is one without a spot, blemish or wrinkle. It must be holy. Holiness is a very vital aspect of being a Christian and especially for the Bride of Christ. What health is to the body, holiness is to the inner person.

Fundamentally, holiness is a cutting off, or separation, from what is unclean and a consecration to what is pure.

Webster's 1828 Dictionary defines it this way: "HOLINESS, n. from holy. It is the state of being holy; purity or integrity of moral character; freedom from sin; sanctity. Applied to the Supreme Being, holiness denotes perfect purity or integrity of moral character, one of his essential attributes. Who is like thee, glorious in holiness? (see Exodus15).

1. Applied to human beings, holiness is purity of heart or dispositions; sanctified affections; piety; moral goodness, but not perfect.

2. Sacredness; the state of any thing hallowed, or consecrated to God or to His worship; applied to churches or temples.

3. That which is separated to the service of God. Israel was holiness unto the Lord (Jeremiah 2)."

It is the combination of anointing and glory that removes all spots, blemishes and wrinkles. Why not make a conscious effort to decide that, from this day forward, you will strive to live a holy, upright and righteous life before the day of your wedding ceremony with Christ. Make a point to live holy from the heart and seek His face daily. We have to be prepared ahead of time for the day we walk down the aisle and look into the face of our Bridegroom, Christ. The wedding banquet prepared afterwards is going to be a one-of-a-kind experience. All are invited but not everyone will be attending. Many are called, but few are chosen. Will your name be engraved on the invitation? Esther prepared herself; and let us now do as she did, and make it a priority to prepare for our Heavenly Bridegroom.

CHAPTER

3

THE BRIDAL COMPANY IN RUTH

In the midst of all that is going on in the world spiritually, economically and politically, the Lord has been stirring my heart like never before with revelation concerning His beloved Bride. We are moving into the last days of the church age where the great harvest and a great purifying will take place. God is preparing for His Son a Bride without spot or blemish. There will be no one allowed in that glorious Bridal company without being washed in the precious blood of Jesus and wearing the robes of His pure, redemptive righteousness. Passion and excitement surge through my spirit as I write of such wonderful things!

Just as Esther had given us beautiful insights into our relationship with Jesus Christ, so also the book of Ruth shows us secrets of intimacy with the Lord. God is preparing a Bride for His Son to bring to the wedding feast of the Lamb. God's ultimate purpose is to have a glorious Church without spot or wrinkle, filled with Christians who have been purified to worship Him in spirit and in truth. The Lord has given me insight in reading through the book of Ruth. The Lord has revealed characteristics of His Bride throughout each chapter of this incredible little book in the Bible.

1. The Determined Bride - Ruth 1:18

Ruth was consumed with a notable desire, determination and convincing love for her bridegroom. She was willing to prove her love to him. Ruth had a determination to leave her past behind in order to gain her future, just like Esther did. Many times we have to leave all we know; for that which we do not know in order to gain the proper perspective and to reach our destination and destiny in God. It seems that God always had a special destiny for His wonderful chosen people. Hallelujah!

2. The Destitute Bride - Ruth 1:20-21

Naomi had found that she was without any friends and had become bitter. When we find ourselves in a situation where all seems hopeless and there is no one to share with, we tend to feel like we have become destitute. In the book of Ruth, we find all three women who were brides were now all destitute. The oldest one, Naomi becomes bitter, Ruth becomes better and Orpah becomes a quitter. Naomi returns back home to Bethlehem with Ruth, but Orpah returns back to her home in Moab. Do your circumstances make you bitter, better or a quitter?

> *Ruth had a determination to leave her past behind in order to gain her destiny*

And she said unto them, Call me not Naomi, call me Mara: for the Almighty hath dealt very bitterly with me. I went out full, and the LORD hath brought me home again empty: why then call ye me Naomi, seeing the LORD hath testified against me, and the Almighty hath afflicted me (Ruth 1:20-21)?

3. The Divine Destiny of the Bride - Ruth 2:19

Ruth does not want to sit around and be taken care of, because she has a destiny to get out into the field and do the work of the Kingdom. The Bride of Christ is not a lazy Bride, but an industrious, conscientious bride that is willing to be obedient to the Lord's call to do His work. It was not just Ruth's ability to do the work, but it was her availability that made her exceptional among the rest of God's people. Are you known for being available for the work of the Lord?

> *God has a divine destiny for each one of us that we must be willing to step into*

And her [Naomi] mother-in-law said unto [Ruth] her, where hast thou gleaned today? And where wroughtest thou? Blessed be he that did take knowledge of thee. And she shewed her mother-in-law with whom she had wrought, and said, the man's name with whom I wrought today is Boaz (Ruth 2:19).

Ruth had a divine destiny that only God could have orchestrated in her life. We see how she was divinely directed by God, as she was led from Moab to Bethlehem.

And Ruth the Moabitess said unto Naomi, "Let me now go to the field, and glean ears of corn after him in whose sight I shall find grace." And she said unto her, "Go, my daughter" (Ruth 2:2).

God has a divine destiny for each one of us as well, and we must be willing to step into our divine destiny where God is placing us. God does not look at just the highly educated for a position that He needs to be filled for His work. God does not call the qualified, but He qualifies the call. Each of us has a very unique DNA - Divine Nature Assignment.

4. The Diligent Bride – Ruth 2:12

In this way, the Bride will be able to provide for her household before the Bridegroom takes her, and then He will take care of her. The ministry of Ruth will surely continue until the end of the Wheat Harvest. She is very diligent in what she is doing at this stage. Continuing in the prophetic picture, we see that Ruth, through her faith and diligence, will be married to Boaz.

> The Lord recompense thy work, and a full reward be given thee of the Lord God of Israel, under whose wings thou art come to trust (Ruth 2:12).

Boaz was a godly man and exhibited an impeccable integrity to those who worked for him in his fields. Boaz recognized Ruth's hard work and her love for her mother-in-law, Naomi, and that distinguished Ruth from all the rest of the gleaners. As the Bride of Christ, we will be set apart from the Body of Christ. Ruth was in the right place at the right time and found the right man.

5. The Intimate Bride - Ruth 3:9

Ruth is craving a closeness and a covering from the man of God. Ruth was willing to do anything in order to prepare herself for being in the presence of Boaz. Ruth was willing to listen to Naomi's advice and she was obedient in that she went and lay at the feet of Boaz. We, too, must be willing to be obedient and be willing to sit at the feet of Jesus, our Heavenly Bridegroom. Sanctification and preparation will become the highest priority as one prepares to become His intimate bride. Are you preparing to be His Bride?

And it came to pass at midnight, that the man was afraid, and turned himself: and, behold, a woman lay at his feet. And he said, Who art thou? And she answered, I am Ruth thine handmaid: spread therefore thy skirt over thine handmaid; for thou art a near kinsman (Ruth 3:8-9).

6. The Eternal Bride - Ruth 4:13,22

Ruth is not caught up in the temporal things of this world but sees her eternal place and destiny. The Bride must anticipate not only the wedding, but more importantly, the role that will follow. Our place with Jesus in eternity will be as His Heavenly Bride forever. There is something very essential that we must know as the Bride of Christ: we have been made complete. The Father's plan was that we complete one another and not compete with each other!

So Boaz took Ruth, and she was his wife: and when he went in unto her, the LORD gave her conception, and she bare a son. And Obed begat Jesse, and Jesse begat David (Ruth 4:13, 22).

Be encouraged in this Scripture and allow the Holy Spirit to move on your heart with divine revelation of where we are as the Church in preparation for our eternal place as His Bride. How is God moving on your heart concerning the Bride?

Ruth, a descendant of Moab, is a Bible character that exhibits Bridal characteristics. Ruth, whose name means "friend or companion," appears a total of 13 times in Scripture. She was the "daughter of Naomi" – prophetically meaning she "had the characteristics of Naomi." The name Naomi means "my delight," and comes from a word meaning "beauty" and "pleasant." This is characteristic and a prophetic picture of Ruth herself and also of the Bride (See Song of Solomon 7:6).

The first Bridal characteristic of Ruth, and the one that makes her stand out most notably, can be seen in the following passage:

> And Ruth said, "Entreat me not to leave thee, or to return from following after thee: for whither thou goest, I will go; and where thou lodgest, I will lodge: thy people shall be my people, and thy God my God: Where thou diest, will I die, and there will I be buried: the LORD do so to me, and more also, if ought but death part thee and me." When she saw that she was steadfastly minded to go with her, then she left speaking unto her (Ruth 1:16-18).

It is here that Ruth's actions reveal her steadfast commitment and devotion to God. Her devotion to God most assuredly qualifies her as one that the Bridegroom would single out as "My delight." Again, she was obedient to go on a path that led her to become an ancestor of Jesus. When Ruth allowed God to show her the destiny that was before her, she became a heroine, not only to her mother-in-law, but to many other women down through the centuries. **It was a leap of faith in order that Ruth could reap from her faith.**

Barley and Wheat Harvests

As we look further at Ruth, we see more of her actions that exhibit some very revealing Bridal characteristics:

> So she kept fast by the maidens of Boaz to glean unto the end of barley harvest and of wheat harvest; and dwelt with her mother in law (Ruth 2:23).

Ruth gleaned through to the end, of both the barley harvest and of the wheat harvest, a prophetic picture of the Bride's work of proclaiming Truth, of preparing the Way, and of gathering souls during barley harvest, and even during the time of the wheat harvest. Barley and wheat are mentioned together in 13 separate Scripture passages, attesting again to these important bridal features revealed by Ruth. We understand that the Bride's work includes gleaning –

of searching for, finding, and gathering of the Scriptural food – for herself. Likewise, the Bride's work includes giving the food she has gathered to those of her household. We then notice, however, that her gleaning continued, not just to the end of barley harvest, but unto the end of the "barley harvest and of the wheat harvest." This shows that she had steadfast endurance till the end. There is a Greek word that describes that steadfast endurance and that is *hupomeno*, (hoop-om-en'-o): to stay under (behind), i.e. remain; figurative to undergo, i.e. bear (trials), have fortitude, persevere:- abide, endure, (take) patient (-ly), suffer, tarry behind.[3]

> *It was not just Ruth's ability to do the work, but it was her availability*

The Bride of Christ will have to have that same endurance until all the harvest is gathered and many souls will be won for the Kingdom of God. We must be willing to work hard and bring the lost ones into the Body of Christ. This is an example relating to that steadfast endurance, and we will have the fortitude and perseverance for this calling of God.

Our current understanding is that the wheat harvest begins after the barley harvest is finished. But the barley harvest signifies the coming of the Bridegroom for the Bride! Here we might ask, "How long will the Bride continue to glean and provide for her household, after the Bridegroom comes – until the end of wheat harvest?"

The Comparison of Ruth's Relationship & The Bride of Christ

The steps that Ruth and Boaz take in this relationship are an example to us as to what we must do to prepare and build that deeper relationship with our Lord. We must not ever be satisfied with a mere existence or with living on leftovers, especially not when

---

3 *Strong's Greek & Hebrew Dictionary*, #5728, s.v. "hupomeno"

we can have it all— when we have Him! The Lord will abundantly supply all our needs. We will consider the preparations that Ruth made in order to be the Bride that God wanted her to be for her Boaz.

First of all, Ruth prepared herself to meet Boaz (See Ruth 3), and we identify how Ruth followed in her mother-in-law's advice in order to do this:

1. Wash herself

Ruth's first step was to wash herself: "Wash thyself [Ruth] therefore, and anoint thee, and put thy raiment upon thee, and get thee down to the floor: but make not thyself known unto the man, until he shall have done eating and drinking" (Ruth 3:3).

This was more than just personal hygiene. Naomi was telling Ruth to prepare herself for her wedding. As a Bride of Christ, we will see that if we want to enter into a deeper relationship with our Lord, we must cleanse ourselves.

Having therefore these promises, dearly beloved, let us cleanse ourselves from all filthiness of the flesh and spirit, perfecting holiness in the fear of God (2 Corinthians 7:1).

We will see that whenever we sin, we must pray and ask God to forgive us and cleanse us.

If we confess our sins, he is faithful and just to forgive us our sins, and to cleanse us from all unrighteousness (1 John 1:9).

2. Anoint herself

Ruth's second step was to anoint herself.

Wash thyself therefore, and anoint thee, and put thy raiment upon thee, and get thee down to the floor: but make not thyself known unto the man, until he shall have done eating and drinking (Ruth 3:3).

These anointings were for a number of different reasons in Biblical times. This particular anointing wasn't for healing, but was to make her more pleasant to be around. The anointing speaks to us of the presence and working of the Holy Spirit, as we have all received the anointing of the Holy Spirit. This is what it communicates to us in 1 John 2:27:

> But the anointing which ye have received of him abideth in you, and ye need not that any man teach you: but as the same anointing teacheth you of all things, and is truth, and is no lie, and even as it hath taught you, ye shall abide in him.

> *It was a leap of faith in order that Ruth could reap from her faith*

The anointing teaches about truth and how we are to abide in Him to prepare us to be His Bride. The more we are like Jesus Christ in our character and our conduct, the more we please our Father. The more we can please our Father, the more He can bless us and use us for His glory as part of the preparation.

3. She changed her clothes and her attitude

Here Ruth was to remove her garments of a widow in sorrow and begin to dress for a joyful wedding. She needed to see herself as a Bride – not as a widow. It is time for a transformation. There are too many times we let our past determine our future. Ruth was now looking toward her future. We must look forward with great anticipation to the day when we will be with our Bridegroom, Jesus.

As believers, we are to always put off the old and put on the new. It is very simply stated in 2 Corinthians 5:17. We must not complicate God's plan for each one of us. We cannot come into God's presence in our own righteousness. We can only come in the righteousness of Jesus Christ and this is an important aspect in the preparation.

> Therefore if any man be in Christ, he is a new creature: old things are passed away; behold, all things are become new (2 Corinthians 5:17).

4. She prepared herself by learning how to present herself to Boaz

Ruth gained a lot of wisdom from her godly mother-in-law. Naomi told her precisely what she needed, to present herself to Boaz in the right way.

> And it shall be, when he lieth down, that thou shalt mark the place where he shall lie, and thou shalt go in, and uncover his feet, and lay thee down; and he will tell thee what thou shalt do (Ruth 3:4).

All that she was doing was unusual for us, but there was nothing improper about this procedure Ruth carried out. It was the way for her to present herself to her kinsman redeemer. Had Ruth used another technique with Boaz, it might have been confusing to him, and he would not have known how to respond to her. God has instructed us on how we are to approach the Lord, and it may seem unusual to others; but the Word of God makes it very clear and we must follow His procedure.

> Let us therefore come boldly unto the throne of grace, that we may obtain mercy, and find grace to help in time of need (Hebrews 4:16).

According to Ruth 3:5, she promised to obey: "And she said unto her, 'All that thou sayest unto me I will do.'" Ruth was very willing to obey what she had been told. We must remember that if we enter into a deeper intimate relationship with the Lord, we must be willing to do what He instructs us to do in His Word. An observation shows us that Ruth was willing to do all that she had been told to do. The will of God is not like a cafeteria where we can pick and choose what we like. God expects us to accept *all* that He plans for us and to obey Him completely.

5. Ruth submitted to Boaz.

Here we see Ruth's submission to Boaz:

And she went down unto the floor, and did according to all that her mother-in-law bade her. And when Boaz had eaten and drunk, and his heart was merry, he went to lie down at the end of the heap of corn: and she came softly, and uncovered his feet, and laid her down. And it came to pass at midnight, that the man was afraid, and turned himself: and, behold, a woman lay at his feet. And he said, "Who art thou?" And she answered, "I am Ruth thine handmaid: spread therefore thy skirt over thine handmaid; for thou art a near kinsman" (Ruth 3:6-9).

Boaz was found at the threshing floor guarding his harvested grain. The threshing floor was usually a raised platform on a hillside somewhere outside the village. The sheaves would be placed on the floor and the grain separated from the stalks. The workers would then throw the grain into the air and let the wind blow away the chaff. The grain would then be heaped together for marketing or for storage. The work would carry on through the night and the men would sleep near the floor to protect their harvest. The Church also must protect the Bride from being stolen from the enemy. The Bride is of great value to her husband.

Visualize how Ruth placed herself at the feet of Boaz. This was also representative of her positioning herself in submission to Him, as her husband. This will correspond to the Scripture of Ephesians 5:22-24:

> Wives, submit yourselves unto your own husbands, as unto the Lord. For the husband is the head of the wife, even as Christ is the head of the Church: and he is the saviour of the body. Therefore as the Church is subject unto Christ, so let the wives be to their own husbands in every thing.

In order to develop that deeper and more intimate relationship with our Lord, we must be willing to submit ourselves unto Him. Submission is a heart issue for each one of us. Ruth's actions and her requests were completely understood by Boaz, as she was presenting herself to become his wife. This was common in those days and Ruth no longer considered herself to be Ruth, the Moabitess; she was now Ruth, the handmaiden of Boaz. It brings to mind Isaiah 43:18, "Remember ye not the former things, neither consider the things of old." We need to see ourselves the way the Lord sees us – as His Bride.

6. Ruth listened to Boaz.

Chapter 3 of Ruth has much more information that is essential to the Bride. Let's contemplate what Ruth 3:10-14 is communicating to us.

> And he said, "Blessed be thou of the LORD, my daughter: for thou hast shewed more kindness in the latter end than at the beginning, inasmuch as thou followedst not young men, whether poor or rich. And now, my daughter, fear not; I will do to thee all that thou requirest: for all the city of my people doth know that thou art a virtuous woman. And now it is true that I am thy near kinsman: howbeit there is

a kinsman nearer than I. Tarry this night, and it shall be in the morning, that if he will perform unto thee the part of a kinsman, well; let him do the kinsman's part: but if he will not do the part of a kinsman to thee, then will I do the part of a kinsman to thee, as the LORD liveth: lie down until the morning." And she lay at his feet until the morning: and she rose up before one could know another. And he said, "Let it not be known that a woman came into the floor."

In Boaz's response to Ruth's request, we see how the Lord responds to us when we endeavor to have that deeper fellowship and companionship with Him. He accepts her as well as us, as we see in verse 10 of Ruth chapter 3.

Boaz could have refused to have anything to do with Ruth, but in his love for her, he accepted her. It is in the same way that the Lord accepts us as we draw nearer to Him. God never wants His children to have a spirit of rejection in their lives. Ruth now experiences that acceptance because of the way Boaz satisfied her, as it says in Ruth 3:11:

> *We need to see ourselves the way the Lord sees us – as His Bride*

And now, my daughter, fear not; I will do to thee all that thou requirest: for all the city of my people doth know that thou art a virtuous woman.

Not only did Boaz calm Ruth's fears, but he also made a promise to her concerning her future. We can relate to what Boaz told her in Ruth 3:11. It is in the darkness that Ruth could not see his face, but she heard his voice when Boaz says for her to "Fear not." That gave her assurance that was not in her feelings or in her circumstances, but in His word. The Lord gives us that same re-assurance when we hear His voice speaking to us. We cannot trust our feelings or our circumstances; but we can fully trust that the Lord is looking out for our best interests in providing for us.

Boaz had a preparedness to promptly adhere with the known will of God, and to encourage the highest good for Ruth, and especially of the poor and needy. It was because he knew her need and prepared her for his choice blessings. The Lord does the same for each of us, as He always wants His choice blessings for His Bride as well. God assures us through His Word that He will finish whatever He starts. The Scripture of Philippians 1:3-6 is for each of us:

> I thank my God upon all my remembrance of you, always in every supplication of mine on behalf of you all making my supplication with joy, for your fellowship in furtherance of the gospel from the first day until now; being confident of this very thing, that he who began a good work in you will perfect it until the day of Jesus Christ.

7. Boaz redeems Ruth as his bride.

This is the moment we all have been waiting for in this story. It is in this part of the story that we witness the function and significance of the kinsman redeemer, Boaz. He will fulfill his obligation and re-assures Ruth that he will do this in the correct and lawful way.

> "And now it is true that I am a near kinsman; howbeit there is a kinsman nearer than I. Tarry this night, and it shall be in the morning, that if he will perform unto thee the part of a kinsman, well; let him do the kinsman's part: but if he will not do the part of a kinsman to thee, then will I do the part of a kinsman to thee, as Jehovah liveth: lie down until the morning." And she lay at his feet until the morning. And she rose up before one could discern another. For he said,

"Let it not be known that the woman came to the threshing floor" (Ruth 3:12-14).

What had seemed to Naomi to be a simple procedure has now turned out to be much more complicated. Although Boaz was a near kinsman and willing to redeem Ruth, there was a nearer kinsman who would need to be considered. This shows that Boaz was an upright businessman and was honest in his dealings even if it meant giving up what he wanted most in life and that was to marry Ruth. Boaz's foremost and primary concern was for Ruth's redemption. We too realize that there is no one other than Jesus Christ who could redeem the lost world; and we are a part of that redemption because He has redeemed us.

We witness to the fact that Ruth now receives gifts from Boaz. Here we see Ruth being the recipient of material gain from Boaz.

"Also," he said, "Bring the vail that thou hast upon thee, and hold it." And when she held it, he measured six measures of barley, and laid it on her: and she went into the city. And when she came to her mother in law, she said, "Who art thou, my daughter?" And she told her all that the man had done to her. And she said, "These six measures of barley gave he me; for he said to me, 'Go not empty unto thy mother in law'" (Ruth 3:15-17).

The gift of grain was supposedly for Naomi, and it is conveyed that six measures of barley would be more than two weeks supply of grain for the both of them. Boaz's gifts to Ruth were just getting better and better because of the favor he was bestowing on Ruth.

He started showing kindness by even sharing his meal with her when she was working in his fields. Also, he sent her home with a half a bushel of grain, much of which was left on purpose for her, and he also now sends her home with about two bushels of barley. This shows that Boaz was a very giving and generous man toward Ruth.

As the Bride of Christ, we too can see how God gives us many gifts of His Spirit so we can share with others. He showers us with His grace and favor when we have that deeper, intimate relationship with Him.

A gift of redemption was for Ruth from Boaz, the kinsman-redeemer. It is observed by Naomi when she asks, "Who art thou, my daughter?" It wasn't that Naomi didn't recognize Ruth at this time. Naomi wanted to know if she was still Ruth the Moabitess, or if she was Ruth, the future wife of Boaz. Ruth had done all that was appropriate for her to do and now she must patiently await the event. Boaz, having undertaken this affair, would be sure to administrate it well. How much more should we, who are true believers, cast our cares and concerns on God, because He has promised to care for each of us.

8. Boaz now completes his duty as a kinsman-redeemer.

It is in patience that Ruth will see the completed work through Boaz. We see it is through faith and patience that she inherits the promises of Boaz as well as the promises of God. Naomi told Ruth to "sit still!" Do you think she might have been excited and it was probably very hard for her to patiently wait for Boaz to make this move? Yet, it tells us in the Scripture that Naomi assured Ruth that Boaz would take care of the matter and that she should wait. One of the hardest things for any of us to do is to wait!

> Then said she, "Sit still, my daughter, until thou know how the matter will fall: for the man will not be in rest, until he have finished the thing this day" (Ruth 3:18).

As the Bride of Christ, we too must wait on the Lord, and allow Him to take care of all the details of us becoming His Bride. We will see the completed work of Jesus is in our lives. Our strength is to sit still and allow the Lord to do His work without us intruding – He does not need our assistance in this process. This statement may encourage us to lay ourselves by faith at the feet of Jesus, because He is our near Kinsman-Redeemer, and having taken our nature upon Himself, He has the right to redeem us just like Boaz did for Ruth. We would do well to seek to receive from Him His directions for our life and to say to the Lord: "Lord, what wilt thou have me to do?"

It is in 1 Thessalonians 4:13-18 that it tells us to wait on His timing for Him to return.

> But I would not have you to be ignorant, brethren, concerning them which are asleep, that ye sorrow not, even as others which have no hope. For if we believe that Jesus died and rose again, even so them also which sleep in Jesus will God bring with Him. For this we say unto you by the word of the Lord, that we which are alive and remain unto the coming of the Lord shall not prevent them which are asleep. For the Lord himself shall descend from heaven with a shout, with the voice of the archangel, and with the trump of God: and the dead in Christ shall rise first: Then we which are alive and remain shall be caught up together with them in the clouds, to meet the Lord in the air: and so shall we ever be with the Lord. Wherefore comfort one another with these words.

Now is the time for us be prepared to meet our Lord just as Ruth was prepared to meet her Boaz. We must spend quality and intimate times with the Lord before He returns for us, His Bride. Are you prepared to meet the Lord? Preparation is a very vital key in our relationship.

CHAPTER

4

THE BRIDAL COMPANY IN REBEKAH

Another story in the Old Testament regarding a bride is found in the wonderful story of how Isaac obtained his bride in Genesis 24. There are many truths that will correlate to the Bride of Christ, and we can gain insight into the heart of God through the beautiful story of Rebekah.

Abraham's Faithful Servant Finds Rebekah

The 24th chapter of Genesis begins with Abraham's realization that the time had come for Isaac to be married. Abraham had a slight problem because his only son, Isaac, was the most eligible bachelor in the country. Normally this would be good, but where Abraham and Isaac were living, the only prospective brides were Canaanite women who worshiped false gods.

Something had to be done, and in that time of arranged marriages, Abraham was the one to get things done. You might expect Isaac to go with the servant and pick the woman out for himself, but three times Abraham forbids Isaac to go with the servant to choose his bride. Rather than let Isaac pick one of the local idolatrous ladies, Abraham calls for his servant and gives him a job to go and find a bride for Isaac.

This is a great Old Testament story of Eliezer, who was Abraham's servant, that Abraham sent back to his homeland to get a bride for his son. Abraham gives Eliezer ten camel loads of wealth to purchase a bride for Isaac, the "bride's price." This servant was completely trusted by Abraham to accomplish this task. The man was just a servant and had no wealth of his own! Yet, off he goes for hundreds of miles with a king's ransom and no supervision, and was to be led by the Spirit of God to pick out a wife for Isaac.

What an assignment this must have been for this Eliezer! When he gets to his destined place, he falls down on his face and cries out to God that he might choose the right woman for his master's son. He puts forth a test and Rebekah, the wife to be, passes it in flying colors. Eliezer gives all the wealth of gifts to Rebekah and her father. He is now ready to take her back to Isaac, with never the slightest thing to gain from the journey, other than the knowledge that God had given his master's son a chosen bride. In that only did he rejoice!

Don't settle for second best ... The Lord has a destiny for your life

The servant probably never realized what an important part he played in the destiny of Isaac as well as for Rebekah.

A personal illustration in my own life made me see the story's great significance, as the Lord's servant did what he was called to do to affect Rebekah's destiny. It was 1979, I was about to be married, and the man I was to be married to was not a Christian. But I wanted to be married and have a family. At that time, my blood brother (who is also my spiritual brother) talked to me very frankly about marrying a non-Christian. It was three days before the wedding and the Lord used him to open my eyes to what was about to take place. The decision affected my destiny, as well. I did not go through with the wedding and as a result, I have gone numerous times to teach the Bible in foreign places. That is part of my destiny which would never have happened, had I not seen the Lord using my brother to affect the destiny in my life. It is at this point, I would say to unmarried Christians: do not settle for second best in your life like I almost did. The destiny the Lord has for you is a most important aspect in your life.

> Then the servant took ten of his master's camels and departed, for all his master's goods were in his hand. And he arose and went to Mesopotamia, to the city of Nahor. And he made his camels kneel down outside the city by a well of water at evening time, the time when women go out to draw water. Then he said, "O LORD God of my master Abraham, please give me success this day, and show kindness to my master Abraham. Behold, here I stand by the well of water, and the daughters of the men of the city are coming out to draw water. Now let it be that the young woman to whom I say, 'Please let down your pitcher that I may drink,' and she says, 'Drink, and I will also give your camels a drink' — let her be the one You have appointed for Your servant Isaac. And by this I will know that You have shown kindness to my master."

> And it happened, before he had finished speaking, that behold, Rebekah, who was born to Bethuel, son of Milcah, the wife of Nahor, Abraham's brother, came out with her pitcher on her shoulder. Now the young woman was very beautiful to behold, a virgin; no man had known her. And she went down to the well, filled her pitcher, and came up. And the servant ran to meet her and said, "Please let me drink a little water from your pitcher." So she said, "Drink, my lord." Then she quickly let her pitcher down to her hand, and gave him a drink. And when she had finished giving him a drink, she said, "I will draw water for your camels also, until they have finished drinking." Then she quickly emptied

her pitcher into the trough, ran back to the well to draw water, and drew for all his camels. And the man, wondering at her, remained silent so as to know whether the LORD had made his journey prosperous or not.

So it was, when the camels had finished drinking, that the man took a golden nose ring weighing half a shekel, and two bracelets for her wrists weighing ten shekels of gold . . . (Genesis 24:10-22, NKJV).

Abraham's servant portrays the servant God desires in the Body of Christ today. God is looking for those who will bring forth a Bride for Jesus to marry; one that is without spots or bruises or any type of blemish. For this purpose, He also seeks servants who will not take the Bride's price and spend it on themselves or spend it foolishly. He will use those who will not take the Bride out into the desert and tarnish her for their own pleasures or their own agenda. He makes use of those who will not try to set up their own kingdom with the Father's wealth, but are good stewards of all that is given into their hands and will see that all goes toward the bringing forth of the Bride for God's Son; for His good pleasure rather than for their own gain. For these servants who share the Father's heart, it is reward enough to do the Lord's will in order to assist someone else to obtain their destiny in God.

God is looking for those who will bring forth a Bride for Jesus to marry

For thousands of years, as this story has been told and retold, the faithful have never doubted that God's angel, a holy matchmaker, played a most important part in the history of Israel and in one of the most beautiful love stories of all time. This love story unfolds in an admirable and enthralling way that only the Lord could have orchestrated in bringing a bride to Isaac. It is a story that will engage your heart from the beginning to the end in an exciting adventure of following the Lord's guiding hand.

It was evening and Eliezer was by the village well because this was the time the women came to draw water. Boldly Eliezer prayed, "O Lord, God of my master Abraham, give me success today and show kindness to my master Abraham. See, I am standing beside this spring, and the daughters of the townspeople are coming out to draw water. May it be when I say to a girl, 'Please let down your jar that I may have a drink,' and she says, 'Drink, and I will water your camels too'—— let her be the one you have chosen for your servant Isaac" (see Gen. 24:13 ff).

It was surely providential that Eliezer had his eyes open as he prayed, because before he had finished, a beautiful young woman came along with a jar on her shoulder. When Eliezer politely asked her for a drink, she not only complied but drew water for his camels as well. So far, we see that his mission is about to be accomplished. Hidden in this simple request for a drink was a prophetic invitation for her. When she made her offer, Rebekah didn't know there was another man that would be involved. All she saw were thirsty camels.

So often, the Holy Spirit comes and asks for just a drink of water and so often, we reject His prophetic invitation because we don't know what's concealed. **It was then concealed, but God's plan was about to be revealed.** But who was she? She needed to be a part of Abraham's clan. Hoping against hope, Eliezer asked the 64,000-shekel question. Her name was Rebekah. She was not only in the clan, but a grand-niece of Abraham, which made her a perfect choice to be a bride for Isaac. Isn't God good the way He orchestrates His plan?

Everything seemed to be falling into place, but Eliezer knew there were still two big problems: Would Rebekah agree to marry Isaac? Would her family allow her to leave and go to Canaan?

There was no guarantee, but by now Eliezer was almost ready to bet the family farm. He gave the astonished Rebekah three pieces of gold jewelry and Rebekah invited him home to meet the family. The extravagant gift of gold jewelry to Rebekah was a clue that something unusual was happening, but her family tactfully did not ask questions. That could wait until after dinner. But Eliezer was excited; he could hardly wait to begin his journey back home. "I will not eat until you have heard what I have to say," he insisted. Then the whole amazing story became, in reality, what God was revealing not only to her, but to others as well.

The family of Rebekah listened with amazement. Eliezer shared how Abraham was persuaded beyond a doubt that the Lord would send His angel and make this servant's journey a success. He also retold the improbable chain of events that had led him to the right geographical spot, how Rebekah appeared while he was still praying, and how she passed Eliezer's test.

Could there be any doubt, with these strange twists of circumstances, that God had chosen Rebekah to be a bride for Isaac? The family answered, "This is of the Lord! Here is Rebekah. Take her and let her become Isaac's wife, as the Lord has directed." Rebekah said, "I will go."

Rebekah gives to us the model of the willing bride. She was not just willing and wanting to marry the first guy that came along. Rather, she is willing to serve someone in need, even though she has never met him before. Rebekah was willing to leave her comfort zone. She was willing to go into times of isolation. She didn't understand the terrain; she was totally dependent on the servant. Others didn't understand how the Lord was leading her into her divine nature assignment. But all of this was part of the wilderness; and in this journey the servant was saying, "Are you willing to follow me?" This man was only a servant, but Rebekah truly loved to help people who were weary.

When Rebekah got out of her bed that day, she probably did not know there would be an opportunity to help someone. She was not prejudiced as to whom she would help. She had a good heart of love and compassion for anyone in need. Rebekah had a heart for doing what she knew was right and she did things enthusiastically and with joy. There is joy in doing the Lord's will and work, no matter how mundane the tasks that have been set before us – even if it means just giving a man a drink and watering his camels.

> *Rebekah gives to us the model of the willing bride*

Notice the simple test which Eliezer placed before Rebekah. She must volunteer to water ten camels and the servants of Abraham. The wells in the Middle East at that time, many of which still exist to this day, were hand-dug and were excavated with a spiral staircase in their walls that allowed the dirt to be hauled out, as well as the water when it was completed. Many of these wells were more than 100 feet deep. That was a task in itself and it certainly wasn't an easy one!

Now let's figure that a thirsty camel could drink at least ten gallons and that the men also drank a minimum of three gallons after their trek across the desert. The water jars that the women carried held about three gallons and would have weighed about thirty pounds (the same as about four gallons of milk) when they were full. The total volume of water this dear woman with a servant's heart carried out of the well that day was about 103 gallons. It figures this way: 103/3 = about 34 trips into that well carrying out thirty pounds each trip. Do you get the picture here? This was no small test even though it seemed like a simple request. It was amazing the strength in this woman when we see it with these statistics. What a woman this servant found in Rebekah!

The name Rebekah has the meaning "captivating," implying "breath-taking" or also "enchanting" which probably implied the impression she made on men. Although Eliezer never set beauty above character or looks above grace, Rebekah was a beautiful woman. It was also interesting that the servant gave Rebekah a nose ring that was a half shekel of gold (and you body-piercing types thought you had a new fad!). This also was the price to be paid to the priests for the redemption of a man (see Exodus 30:11-13).

Now Isaac is found contemplating, or maybe daydreaming, when he sees something in the distance. He noticed not the woman, but the camels. Remember that. As they near, the woman asks the servant, "Is this the master?" "Yes," he says. She covers her face with a veil. The servant tells Isaac about the miracles God did to bring the woman there. Isaac accepts and loves her and she becomes his bride.

Rebekah, one of the four matriarchs of Judaism, was destined to become a great woman, as God's hand was on her. Her destiny started when she said she was willing to go and be Isaac's bride. She had somehow kept herself, in spite of her beauty, for the right man. She was a virgin, untainted, pure in every respect—a worthy bride for the heir to Abraham's great, divine blessing. God had ordered her steps and He ordered her stops.

At the right time God will send His Spirit to find a suitable bride—not an idolatrous woman, but a woman from "our own family." This woman is to be a selfless servant. The Spirit meets her at the place where everyone draws living water (the Word of God) and compels her to follow Him into a life of dedication and to trust unreservedly. He gives her gifts of the Spirit of God. The woman God wants will be a woman who is in the Word of God and who freely shares the Word with total strangers as part of the harvest.

In turn, men are to be as Isaac, found "in the field" of evangelism which is so white ready for the harvest. Men are to be meditating and praying that God sends more workers into the field.

Therefore," said he unto them, The harvest is great, but the laborers are few: pray ye therefore the Lord of the harvest, that he would send forth laborers into his harvest (Luke 10:2).

In fact, it says that Isaac was at a place called, *Beer Lahai-Roi*, which means, "The well of God's vision for life." The man of God is to drink from God's vision for life. He waters the world with God's way of life, Jesus Christ and the Holy Spirit. Rebekah first saw her husband Isaac by another well, the well Lahai-Roi where he was awaiting her arrival. We must believe by faith that when we open our Bible to study, the Holy Spirit is there to lead us to Jesus, and that Jesus is alive and sees us as we come daily to draw fresh water. As we abide in His Word and He abides in us, we will eventually see Him face-to-face. We see Rebekah coming to Isaac and Isaac going out to meet his bride. There is coming a glorious day when the Lord will come and meet His wonderful Bride as well.

> *God had ordered her steps and He ordered her stops*

When the woman has been led far enough away from her attachments to the former life, then the Spirit will lead her into view where she become noticed by the man of God. What Isaac, the man of God, sees first is not the figure of the woman, but the method of her travel: as Isaac observed his own camels at a distance, the man of God would see that the Lord was providing him with the woman as one of his gifts from Him.

Rebekah asks the servant, "Is this the man?" He says, "Yes" and she prepares herself by covering her outward beauty with godly humility. The Spirit brings her closer to the man of God and tells him to look at this woman who has left everything behind to follow Him into the pursuit of God's will. Look at how she has crossed a desert of trials, riding upon the gifts of the Spirit. This woman is chosen by God to be the wife of whomever the Father desires and she has proven herself to be a servant of all, a traveler and a sojourner. Isaac just had to accept her and love her. And so, the 24th chapter of Genesis ends with the words, "Isaac loved Rebekah."

Our Father God will send His Spirit at the appropriate time to prepare wives for His sons. Until then, men must be wholeheartedly in the fields of evangelism and prayer. When she does arrive, the man will know because of two things: he will see her riding upon the gifts of the Spirit instead of walking in her own strength. And the Spirit Himself will testify in the man's heart that God the Father has selected and prepared her, having first proven her worth as a helper by testing her willingness to serve strangers with the Word of Life.

This story has a beautiful lesson for the Church today. The redeemed of the Lord will have a servant's heart and those who serve the Bride of Christ do so without wanting anything for themselves. Their whole joy of serving is to see the Son gain His spotless Bride and dwell together with her for eternity.

This story portrays a greater story of how God sent His own servant, the Holy Spirit, to draw the Church from the world, a Bride for His only Son. When she responded, her heart was transformed and became as virgin soil, tilled and watered for the seed of life to awaken within her. The life she carried in her heart as the heir to God's blessing would

But we all, with unveiled face beholding as in a mirror the glory of the Lord, are changed into the same image from glory to glory . . .

84

ultimately emerge as she drew near to her King, even though she was veiled. The veil implies partial sight, the obscuring of truth through our humanity. But when we finally come before Him, the veil is taken away.

> Nevertheless when one shall turn to the Lord, the veil shall be taken away. Now the Lord is that Spirit: and where the Spirit of the Lord is, there is liberty. But we all, with unveiled face beholding as in a mirror the glory of the Lord, are changed into the same image from glory to glory, even as by the Spirit of the Lord (2 Corinthians 3:16-18).

CHAPTER

5

THE BRIDAL COMPANY IN THE NEW TESTAMENT

In the New Testament, there is a parable of the ten virgins and their oil. Let's look at how this story pertains to the Bride of Christ. The parable has nothing to do with the virgin's salvation, or their new birth; but it has everything to do with their walk with the Lord and the catching away of the Bride!

We need to pay attention to this parable, if we are to comprehend the thought of being prepared as a Bride of Christ. Especially see how the application of the virgins that were with oil will be pertinent for the days of darkness that may be in the future for each of us. This is a day of testing and trials for God's people. In fact, we might say we are living in a day in which God is revealing the hearts of men and the Lord is uncovering the insufficiencies like that of the Laodicean Church. They profess to be rich and filled with oil, and have need of nothing. Yet, the Lord is revealing their insufficiency.

Today, our confidence in experiences, in blessings, in gifts, in ministries, etc. – all are going to fail us. These days, the people of God generally find it easy to come up with solutions to solve our problems. They have access to a vast library of success books, seminars and workshops - all promising personal spiritual enlightenment, as well as the enhancement of church life and church growth. The standard seems to be: Does it work? If it works and at least seems to perform the desires of our hearts – that seems to be all that is important. Whether or not it is God's way does not seem to be important, especially as long as it will bring forth God's objective.

> *All ten of the virgins received the same invitation and the same instruction –*
> *PREPARE*

In our culture, we think of the word "virgin" as meaning sexually pure. However, in the Bible, the Greek word for "virgin" only means "unmarried daughters." A virgin in the Bible, may or may not be chaste or pure, though it is usually virginity that is a sign of purity.

In studying this parable that Jesus shares in Matthew 25, there are two categories of virgins that make up the family of God: foolish ones and wise ones. These ten virgins represent the body of the Church. They all profess to know the Lord Jesus as their personal Savior. Further, they have all experienced true Christian salvation. All ten of the virgins received the same invitation and the same instruction – PREPARE. Although they are both a part of the Body of Christ, they have a very different destiny.

> Then shall the kingdom of heaven be likened unto ten virgins, which took their lamps, and went forth to meet the bridegroom. And five of them were wise, and five were foolish. They that were foolish took their lamps, and took no oil with them: But the wise took oil in their vessels with their lamps. And at midnight there was a cry made, Behold, the bridegroom cometh; go ye out to meet him. Then all those virgins arose, and trimmed their lamps. And the foolish said unto the wise, Give us of your oil; for our lamps are gone

out. But the wise answered, saying, Not so; lest there be not enough for us and you: but go ye rather to them that sell, and buy for yourselves. And while they went to buy, the bridegroom came; and they that were ready went in with him to the marriage: and the door was shut (Matthew 25:1-11).

This parable is one of the best known and is probably the least understood of all the parables. It is a parable that has been intriguing for years. Let's take a closer look at some of the details and see if we can bring this into focus.

Who are these virgins and what happens to them? All are called virgins. All of them are waiting for the Bridegroom to arrive. All of them get tired and fall asleep. All of them hear the call and wake up. All of them trim their lamps. All of them have some oil in their lamps. The foolish do not have enough oil and they have to go to buy more oil. They did not properly prepare and while the foolish are on their way to get more oil, the Bridegroom comes and takes the wise ones. When the foolish return they are locked out.

Notice that all ten of the virgins had lamps that were to light their way in times of darkness. Psalm 119:105 says, "Thy word is a lamp unto my feet, and a light unto my path." Not only are all of these individuals virgins, but we will also be identifying them as part of the family of God. They all had lamps (the Word of God) which, when used, brings enlightenment. It is clear that, in this parable, they were all believers.

Five Virgins are Wise, Five Virgins Are Foolish

And five of them were wise, and five were foolish (v.2).

What made some of these believers wise and others foolish?

They that were foolish took their lamps, and took no oil with them: But the wise took oil in their vessels with their lamps (v. 3-4).

Very simply, the wise believers took the oil with them wherever they went, and the foolish did not. There is only one way that we can maintain the oil that will provide the light. We will sustain our vision of His appearing and be prepared for that appearing by coming into union with Him and continually keeping our eyes on Jesus. God has an inexhaustible source of oil for each one of us, because it is only God's provision for His people in the hour of famine and of darkness that brings our faith into reality. You must begin to walk in identification and union with Christ, in His Cross as well as in His life. Only in Him is there an unfailing supply. There is not much use of a lamp without fuel. What does that mean? Oil is a type of the Holy Spirit.

The Holy Spirit causes your lamp, the Word of God, to be illuminated as you read it. "But the wise took oil in their vessels with their lamps" (v:4). The Word of Truth is the lamp of the Wise Virgins. "Thy Word is a lamp unto my feet, and a light unto my path" (Psalm 119:105). The godly understand the treasure that the Word of God is – complete with its indwelling author and illuminator. "When He, the Spirit of Truth, is come, He will guide you into all truth" (John 16:13). This oil, the Holy Spirit, causes your life to burn brightly, so that all who are around you can see Jesus, THE LIGHT, in your actions and speech. God's love is the light that shines and permeates the darkness. Jesus is the light of the world and His Bride will be those who reflect that light from within.

The story of the ten virgins reveals some solemn truths for all of us. First, there are some things that just cannot be borrowed. I cannot give my relationship with God, or my faith or trust in God, to anyone else. I can share my faith, but I cannot have my own faith depleted. It is each person's responsibility to have their own personal faith in Jesus.

Second, there are vital things that cannot be had or purchased at the last minute. Knowing God is a lifetime endeavor of building that special relationship with him. God expects us to live up to the light we have been given. Christians who have been slack in their faith, perhaps going to church occasionally but living life with the same worldly standards as nonbelievers, will find themselves suddenly cut off from a relationship with God. It is not that God does not love them, but that they have hardened their hearts toward Him by repeatedly rejecting Him and His ways. Your faith is not going to be built on a crisis situation. It is built on your knowledge of the Word of God and how you live your daily life. When terror strikes, those who don't have oil won't have the faith it takes to know how to find peace in Christ. They will be lost in darkness with no access to God. This has been of their own choosing. God will no longer overlook the sins of those who claim to be His but act otherwise.

> *Thy word is a lamp unto my feet, and a light unto my path*
> ~ *Psalm 119:105*

The betrothal was a Jewish custom that occurred before the consummation of a marriage. Today, we would call it an engagement period, but betrothal was a much deeper commitment than an engagement. During the betrothal period, which was customarily a year, the bride was given all the rights of a wife, including all of her future husband's income and inheritance. It is during this year of betrothal that the bridegroom would prepare a place for his bride to live. Then the day would come when he would call for his bride, and this was done in a unique way.

Every year in the small villages on the Judean hillsides, there were as many as ten virgins or more that could be betrothed. Their duty was to be prepared at all times for the trumpet sound and the shout, "The bridegroom comes!" At that moment, the virgins were to light their lamps so the bridegrooms could find them. Usually the shout would come in the midnight hour. All the bridegrooms would then travel down the hillside to find their respective bride, and thus would begin the time of celebration before the wedding supper and the consummation of their marriages. The virgins would usually know the season of their betrothal, but not know the exact day. They were to always have sufficient oil to keep their lamps ready for that special night.

In this story, five of the anticipatory virgins went out to meet their bridegrooms and they also carried vessels of oil with them. The other five failed to have sufficient oil with them and their lights went out because their bridegrooms tarried for a while. The virgins who were not prepared asked for oil from the prepared virgins, who told them to go out and buy some more oil. While the unprepared were purchasing more oil, the marriage took place and the door was shut to them.

Our bridegroom, Jesus, will be coming very soon and it is our responsibility to stay filled with the oil of the Holy Spirit, so our lights will not go out before He comes for us. We are the only light the world has now, and it seems the darkness around us becomes more intense as we await the coming of our Lord. This is the time for our light to shine – now more than ever, because many are living in gloom and doom. The question for us to ask is, "Are we receiving daily a fresh filling of this oil of anointing from the Holy Spirit?" The Holy Spirit always has sufficient oil, but do we receive it? Daily, I pray this prayer, and you may want to pray it with me: "Lord, I ask for a double portion of Your anointing. Fill me with Your Holy Spirit today and let me not be deceived in my walk with the Lord in any way."

Throughout the Word of God, we are exhorted to walk continually in the Spirit. Ephesians 5:18 commands us "to be filled and keep on being filled with the Spirit." Just because you speak in tongues does not mean that you are continually filled with the Spirit or walking in the Spirit. Having said that, let me make it clear that receiving the baptism of the Holy Spirit and speaking in the heavenly prayer language that God gives you is important. It allows your spirit to speak to the Spirit of the Lord and it can increase the intimacy you have with Him. The more you talk to someone and listen to him or her, the more intimate you become.

Another aspect of continually being filled, is to remember how olive oil is produced. We forget that it is through the shaking and crushing of the olives that oil comes forth. The olive tree that is sometimes very disfigured when you look at the appearance on the outside. We see that even though the trees look beautiful when they are producing many olives, it doesn't produce oil by staying on the tree. In Biblical times, the olives were placed on a huge circular stone with another large stone used to crush them in order to produce the oil.

So many times in our lives we do not understand the shaking that is going on, but it is through the shaking, that the Lord is allowing the squeeze within us in order to make us more productive for the kingdom of God. It is then that we, and others, will see what we have on the inside.

Those With Oil Are Intimate With God

The Bride, the wise virgin with oil in her lamp, is to be continually praying in the Holy Spirit. I believe the whole point of having oil in your lamp is to be intimate with God. Think about this significant fact: If you are filled with the Spirit, the Word will be illuminated to you, as Jesus, THE WORD, speaks to you. Jude 1:20 says, "But ye, beloved, building up yourselves on your most holy faith, praying in the Holy Ghost..." Like anyone who seeks a spouse, Jesus seeks a Bride that really knows Him in an intimate way and not someone who is merely a casual acquaintance.

Many times, Christians start very motivated and on fire but after awhile, allow the things of the world to overtake and entrap them. They grow weary in well doing and a kind of spiritual laziness sets in, as they tend more to the flesh than to the spirit. However, this is a trap and, if you have fallen into it, you will be left behind at the critical time. When you are daily filled, and you continue to be filled with the oil of the Holy Spirit, you will always have enough oil. Just as importantly, continually listen to Him as you apply the oil in your lamp, reading and meditating on the Word day and night. The result is true intimacy with Jesus.

It says in verse 5 of this parable in Matthew 25: "While the bridegroom tarried, they all slumbered and slept." Notice that before the bridegroom comes, both the foolish and the wise virgins are asleep. In Ephesians 5:14, we are exhorted to "Awake thou that sleepest, and arise from the dead, and Christ shall give thee light. See that ye walk circumspectly, not as fools, but as wise."

Observe that after we are told to wake up, there is a reference to the resurrection that accompanies the rapture. The result of our waking up is that we will become wise and will be given light (or illumination) of the Word as to the nearness of the hour of His return. In other words, as we wake up and realize how little time we have left, and begin to really love Jesus, obey His commandments and walk circumspectly; our lamps will be full of oil. They will give off light, making us the wise virgins that Jesus seeks.

The next few verses seem to indicate that there could be an admonition, or warning, that will come right before Jesus comes for His Bride. There is a scriptural study discussing all of the evidence that indicates that those watching will, in the fullness of time, know the season of the rapture right before it occurs.

> And at midnight there was a cry made, Behold, the bridegroom cometh; go ye out to meet him. Then all those virgins arose, and trimmed their lamps. And the foolish said unto the wise, Give us of your oil; for our lamps are gone out. But the wise answered, saying, Not so; lest there be not enough for us and you: but go ye rather to them that sell,

and buy for yourselves. And while they went to buy, the bridegroom came; and they that were ready went in with him to the marriage: and the door was shut (Matthew 25:6-10).

Remember that Noah was given progressive revelation that eventually led to his knowing the exact day that he would be lifted up in the ark a short time before it happened. In the same way, I believe the Bible teaches that those in the Church who are watching and anticipating the Lord's return will receive progressive revelation about the timing of the rapture and eventually, will know the exact day a short time before the rapture. What about the Scripture that says, "No man knows the day and hour"? Do you know that there is another passage in Scripture that says that those who are awake will know this hour? Yet, the Church is now in idleness, or even asleep; and this idleness is very strange behavior for the Church. She is a "bride to be" and must know what it means to be that Bride of Christ. Does the Church really know what this means? The Church is especially called to be a witness for the Bridegroom in this world. She has been chosen into a glorious destiny for such a time as this.

> *When you are daily filled, and you continue to be filled with the oil of the Holy Spirit, you will always have enough oil*

This passage does not say whether the wise virgins knew the exact day, although being intimate with Jesus, it is likely that this information could have been shared only with them. What is certain from this parable is that they were warned a short time before that the coming of their Bridegroom was very, very close.

Trimming the Wick

In the time frame between the warning cry and the appearing of Jesus for His Bride, the first thing that occurs is that all the virgins wake up and proceed to "trim their lamps." Living in a rural area, early in my life I had an idea what "trimming a lamp" meant. A friend that lived in the rural area knew about lamps that were used on occasion if the electricity went out, and he told me that when you trim the wick, two things occur. First, the smoke is eliminated and secondly, the flame burns brighter.

Because the wise virgins had been continually trimming their wicks, their lamp burned brightly

In the parable of the virgins, the wick represents the "world and our fleshly desires." The world must be continually trimmed out of our lives. Also our motives that became polluted, therefore making our light to become dim, should be removed as well. We cannot be our brightest or best example to others, if we allow the world into our lives. Jesus said we must be in the world and not of it (John 17).

Knowing the bridegroom was about to come, all the virgins trimmed their wicks, but with one difference: the foolish virgins had no oil to sustain a flame; the wise virgins did. In other words, the foolish virgins still did not have an intimate relationship with Jesus that results from being continually filled with the Holy Spirit. So, their attempt to suddenly try to be righteous, were only works—not a holiness that springs from walking in the Spirit of God.

Holiness is a quality of the Bride of being without spot and wrinkle (Ephesians 5:27). It is a reflection of the character of the Spirit of God in our lives. In this day and time, we cannot emphasize enough about holiness. The world wants to see a difference in our lives. It is not in our own ability to do good works and avoid sin. The foolish virgins at the last minute tried to cut out the pollution of the world by trying to avoid sin and do righteous acts. But because they were not already walking in the Holy Spirit, having their lamps full of oil, their efforts could not bring forth that passionate flame that Jesus wants His future wife to have. We need to learn this lesson now, so we can have our lamps ready and continually filled with oil.

Because the wise virgins had been trimming their wicks on an ongoing basis, as the Spirit of God would convict them, their lamp burned brightly. They were ready when Jesus came for them. Are you ready for the return of the Lord?

The fact that the foolish virgins have gone to the marketplace to buy oil, for a period of time after the warning cry and before the coming of the Bridegroom, shows that in this parable a warning is given. If this parable does give details of what will happen before Jesus comes to gather His Bride, it could mean just a warning. The point made in this parable, however, is that if you have not developed intimacy with Jesus before that warning is given, then you will not be taken as the Bride when He subsequently comes for His beloved!

The Door is Shut ~ How Does This Fit?

The last part of verse 10, refers to the Bride as the ones who have made themselves ready.

And while they went to buy, the bridegroom came; and *they that were ready* went in with him to the marriage: and the door was shut.

The wise virgins who prepared by taking oil (receiving the Holy Spirit) entered the kingdom. But the foolish virgins who didn't prepare went to look for oil and while they were gone the bridegroom came and "the door was shut." They said, "Lord, Lord open to us." But He answered and said, "Verily I say unto you, I know you not." They had heard that the bridegroom was coming and they called Him "Lord," but they had not prepared.

The key verse that is fundamental to the premise of this book is Revelation 19:7, which says:

Let us be glad and rejoice, and give honor to him: for the marriage of the Lamb has come, and his wife has made herself ready.

If we do not make ourselves ready by doing what is necessary to be the Bride, we will find ourselves foolish virgins shut out at the rapture to face the tribulation.

The Exclamation of the Foolish Virgins

The response of the foolish virgins after they see that they have been left behind, is one of anguish and affliction.

Afterward came also the other virgins, saying, Lord, Lord, open to us. But he answered and said, Verily I say unto you, I know you not (Matthew 25:11-12).

Notice that these foolish virgins address Jesus as "Lord," showing that they are believers. In other words, these are saints—they are saved. So, this has nothing to do with their salvation (if they are born again or not), but it does have a lot to do with their destiny in coming events, as their walk or lack of walk with God will change their personal destinies.

1 Corinthians 12:3 says, "no man can say that Jesus is the Lord, but by the Holy Ghost." But obviously, there is a big difference between calling Jesus "Lord" and actually making Him Lord of their lives. Jesus' response to them was "I know you not." He was not saying that these foolish virgins were never born again, but that they were not intimate with Him. In other words, you never spent time with the Lord. Did you think you spent your time wisely and did you think that your two-hour duty on Sunday gave you an intimacy

with Jesus? How much time and devotion did you give in reading God's Word? Or was your time used in watching television, or just being busy with other priorities? We must remember that "BUSY" is maybe really being under Satan's yoke. This may be a time when you need to evaluate how you spend your time.

The Result of the Closed Door

There were different reactions that Jesus had to the protests, as recorded in the different accounts of their rejection.

And then will I profess unto them, I never knew you: depart from me, ye that work iniquity (Matthew 7:23).

But he answered and said, Verily I say unto you, I know you not (Matthew 25:12).

But he shall say, I tell you, I know you not whence ye are; depart from me, all ye workers of iniquity (Luke 13:27).

> *Let us be glad and rejoice, and give honor to him: for the marriage of the Lamb has come, and his wife has made herself ready*
> Revelation 19:7

Two of the accounts mentioned that Jesus did not know them. We already stated that this refers to Jesus not knowing them intimately. It is not saying that these individuals were never born again. Even in the natural, if you are born into a family, but are separated from them for extended periods of time, it is apparent that your intimacy with them can be affected. Even though you are born again into the family of God, if you separate from Jesus, through your sin for extended

> *Our actions and our thoughts will be affected by our ongoing fellowship as we press in to know Him more*

periods of time, intimacy with Him will be lost. You will hear this statement several times throughout this book: Jesus is coming for a Bride who is totally in love with Him–body, soul and spirit–and that intimacy with the Lord must begin here and now.

In Genesis, it is interesting that when it says, "Adam knew Eve," it was talking about sexual union, the one form of intimacy that unites a husband and wife–body, soul and spirit. For us to be His Bride, we must continually commune with Him, praying spirit to Spirit. Prayer is how we love Him with our spirit. We love Him with our body by putting the Word of God in action. We love Jesus with our soul by keeping our mind, will and emotions focused on Him. Our actions and our thoughts will be affected by our ongoing fellowship, as we press in to know Him more. Our minds have to be informed of the Lord, so we can be transformed into what He wants us to be and we will be then conformed into the image of Christ.

The Destiny or Fate of the Foolish Virgins

In these parallel accounts of those left behind at the arrival of the Bridegroom for His Bride, the fate of these foolish virgins is quite traumatic. Looking back at Matthew 7:23 and Luke 13:27, we see that Jesus tells them in each account to "depart from me, ye that work iniquity." If you are walking in disobedience to Jesus, resulting in unrighteousness, the water of the Word is not washing you. These unrighteous, disobedient, foolish virgins are departed or "parted from," being with Jesus when He comes for His Bride. The rapture separates the wise virgins, who are the Bride and go to be with Jesus, from the foolish who may go through the fires of the tribulation.

100

Both the wise and the foolish hear the Words of God, but only the wise are DOERS of what God tells them! James 2:20 says that faith without works or corresponding actions is dead. The foolish, who have no corresponding actions to the Word that they have heard, are not full of faith, as the wise are. Their faith is considered dead, or inoperative. The members of the Bride truly build their lives upon Jesus, continually feeding on the Word of God. And their house is a place prepared just for them (John 14:1).

In summary, I believe it is safe to assume that all ten virgins are Christians for the following reasons: they are virgins, they are waiting for the Bridegroom, they have oil, and they call Him "Lord." The Bible never refers to them as the lost virgins, just foolish. The foolish are waiting for the Bridegroom, who is Jesus. The lost are not waiting for the return of the Bridegroom; so we see a difference between foolish and lost in this context. The lost do not have a clue about the return of Jesus. There are even a lot of Christians who aren't looking for the Bridegroom, so I would say that all ten are in the category of being born-again Christians.

We also know that there is a warning that goes out just before the Bridegroom comes so they are all awake. The problem is that five are ready and five are not. What's the matter with the foolish? The foolish find out that their lamps are going out due to an insufficient amount of oil. Oil in the Bible is a picture, a symbol, and a type of the Holy Spirit. The foolish were not completely devoid of oil. They had some, but it was just not enough. Their lamps were going out. So what did they do?

The foolish virgins after recognizing their predicament first asked the wise virgins for some of their oil. But the wise virgins said that they only had enough for themselves and they told the foolish to go buy their own. So they left to go get more oil. What happened to the foolish ones? When they returned they found out that those who were ready, the wise, went into the wedding feast and the foolish were locked out. It is a heart-breaking picture. In their desperation they cry out, "Lord, Lord open up for us." This is another indication that these are Christians and we must not delay in preparing for the return of our Bridegroom.

We must always keep check on the source of our supply. The oil of the Lord has never been for sale. Whether it is the oil supply for the lamp in the heavenly temple, or the one in the temple of your heart, it simply is not for sale. We cannot merchandise the anointing of the Holy Spirit in our lives.

Our Divine Assignment is to Keep Our Lamp Burning

Those who know Jesus as Lord and Savior are walking around with the light of Christ within them.

Let us be wise in all that we do to prepare for Him and we will be His Glorious Bride with plenty of oil for these last days

For God, who commanded the light to shine out of darkness, hath shined in our hearts, to give the light of the knowledge of the glory of God in the face of Jesus Christ. But we have this treasure in earthen vessels, that the excellency of the power may be of God, and not of us (2 Corinthians 4:6-7).

Those who know Christ are jars of clay, or as the NKJV says, "earthen vessels." They are clay, or earthen lamps, that shine forth the light of Jesus Christ. This 2 Corinthians verse is clear—it shows the benefit of having the light of Christ, and the horrible fate that awaits those who do not have the light of Christ within them.

While a person is waiting, if he devotes himself wholly to Christ–spending time with Him in His Word and in prayer–that person can help others obtain oil. A person needs to be prepared, for we know not what day we will die or go to be with Him in the rapture. Going to church is not going to save us, but a heart-felt and genuine belief in Jesus Christ as Lord and Savior will.

Our choices these days will allow the oil to increase in our lamps or will cause us to run out of oil, and will keep us running in circles until it is too late. There is still time to obtain oil to keep our lamps lit. Let us be wise in all that we do to prepare for Him and we will be His Glorious Bride with plenty of oil for these last days.

CHAPTER

6

THE PREPARATION TIME IS NOW

Preparation Is A Vital Key

If we are really hearing what the Spirit is saying to the churches in this hour, you are probably aware that we are hearing above all else the word "PREPARE." It is indeed an hour of preparation for the Bride of Christ. God always prepares His people when He is about to do some new thing... and a "new thing" is happening in the earth at this time. God is ushering His Bride into a time of being prepared and adorned. His desire is that she carry His glory and walk in a place of purity and power. When we as the Church walk with the glory of the Father upon us, His Kingdom will be done on earth as it is in Heaven.

We must now begin our own journey as the Bride of Christ. It is a journey to and through the heart of God. The Bride of Christ will have singleness of heart and is content to have that intimate relationship with the Lord. It is from that day forward that we will continue to look for His appearing. Every step of this journey must bring us closer and closer to Him.

God has always been doing new things ever since the beginning of creation. Let us not get distressed at the thought that God might be doing something new just for today. Our God has not exhausted His resources, even when they tell us that God never does anything new. From the time He placed man on the earth, and unto this day, He has been reaching into His own heart of wisdom, knowledge, and truth bringing forth new things. It is encouraging for the Body of Christ to realize what God is doing today.

> For eye hath not seen, nor ear heard, neither have entered into the heart of men, the things which God hath prepared for them that love Him. But God hath revealed them unto us by His Spirit (1 Corinthians 2:9-10).

Has our God finally depleted and consumed all His treasures of wisdom and knowledge upon His people? He has nothing more to say or do but to bring forth the old? Certainly we appreciate how God has worked of old, but the true steward of the mysteries of God will continue to bring forth from his treasures things new and old for God is a God who reserves His very best for His children. Let us recognize the new unfolding of His purposes and designs, new insights into His ways, new glimpses of His glory and presence today. We must be open and teachable to the "new things" in these last days before He takes His Bride home with Him forever.

God is bringing about a transformation. Have you ever distinguished how obviously different the caterpillar and the butterfly are in appearance? They would seem to not be associated in any way, yet they are one and the same creature in different and diverse stages. A spectacular and stunning transformation takes place in the life of this amazing creature. The transformation is so extreme and complete that this creature has two different names. At one period of its existence it is called a caterpillar. At another, it is called a butterfly. What a difference the transformation makes in this creation!

In the same way, God has changed the names of men and women whom He has transformed. For example, Abram became Abraham. Sarai became Sarah. Jacob became Israel. Cephas became Peter. Saul became Paul. Their names were changed after they were transformed by an encounter with God. We all have been changed and/or transformed in some way when we have encountered the Lord in our lives as well. My life is not like it used to be, and thank God that He is still changing me until I can be not only transformed in my life, but I will be conformed into His likeness.

In these last days before the return of Christ, there is another amazing transformation which must take place – A Bride will be fashioned and formed. This Bride will be absolutely radiant without stain or wrinkle. The Bride will be holy and exemplary in her life in every way. This Bride will be awesome to behold and she will be an appropriate Bride for the Son of God. This will all be a part of the plan of God since the beginning of time.

This transformation is in order for the Bride to be disclosed for all to see. It is no less revolutionary than that of the caterpillar into a butterfly. The world will see the conversion and stand in amazement in regard to the Bride of Christ. The Holy Spirit is at work to call forth a Bride out of the Church, to wash her, to transform her, and to assist her in making the necessary preparations to make herself ready.

Some, who read of this transformation will be skeptical. They will look at the caterpillar that the Church now resembles and balk at the prospect of a butterfly coming forth from her. Some will believe it is merely wishful thinking. Others will believe the timing is incorrect and they will believe that the Church will be transformed, but only after the saints get to heaven. There will be those who are being washed by the water of the Word and will find faith arising in their hearts for the future. They will allow the transforming work of God's Spirit to perform miracles in their lives. It is these who will receive a new name. They will be called "the Bride of Christ."

It is appropriate that these receive a new name. They are actually a whole new type of creature. They will be as different from the development of nominal churchgoers and half-hearted confessors of Christ, as the butterfly is different from the caterpillar. They will not be content or satisfied with just salvation and a promise of heaven. They will have a passion to intimately know the One who gave His all for them.

It is this passion that will possess these faithful ones to the path of transformation. The path is laborious and comes at great cost, but the end is glorious and it promises an assured habitation with the Son of God. These faithful ones will not settle for a visitation of God, but are ready for a habitation in God. We want and desire God to inhabit every aspect of our lives and it is not for us to pick and choose what part He resides in each of us. Jesus wants all of us and we want all of Him.

The path is laborious and comes at great cost, but the end is glorious and it promises an assured habitation with the Son of God

There is a definite in-between stage that occurs as a caterpillar begins the process of becoming a butterfly. This stage is most vital. The caterpillar will never become a butterfly without this period of its existence. The caterpillar spins a cocoon around itself and this cocoon becomes a hidden chamber, where the miracle of transformation occurs out of sight.

Outsiders will notice that there doesn't appear to be very much activity in the cocoon. It seems rather odd that caterpillars appear active, butterflies appear active and yet, the cocoon seems to be totally lifeless. It appears as a sign of death. Those who desire the appearance of constant activity will not eagerly enter into the cocoon, or in the Secret Place of the Lord.

Those who seek comfort above conformity to Christ, or who live for the opinions of men, will not willingly enter into this place. It is very uncomfortable, confining, and does not make sense to the world, nor does much of the Church understand its function. Most people in church think that "busyness" is what should be taking place. Busyness is not the business of the Bride of Christ. For these reasons and others, many will shun this place of seeming death and they will forfeit the greater glory and resurrection life that can be attained through this process. It is a time of darkness and feeling that no one cares about their predicament. No one is around to assist them out of that darkness, and they do not care about the outcome either.

The remnant portion of the Body of Christ will follow wherever their Savior leads. This is a cocoon stage, a death process that they must submit to even though the outcome is uncertain. It really is an adventure of stepping out in faith into the unknown. This stage is vital and cannot be skipped over.

It relates to the wilderness portion of the trip from Egypt to the Promised Land of Israel. God will lead all of His children through this part of the journey, but very few will appreciate its significance in preparing them to be a part of the Bride of Christ. Some will not survive this part of the journey. Some will want to turn back to their old ways. It is here that the transformation takes place. So many miss what the preparation is and how vital it is in their walk with the Lord. It is here that flesh is stripped away and a spiritual being arises even though it is a painful process. Many want the end result without going through the process.

As with the butterfly, the Bride of Christ will be prepared in a hidden chamber just like Esther was in the Old Testament. Her transformation will be veiled from the eyes of the world and much of the Church, as well. Then, we will see her emerge and will wonder at the miracle that has taken place. But even in knowing, many will not submit to the process required for the glory of God to be revealed in them.

Love is essential as Jesus leads His Bride through wilderness places, preparing her. Even as a butterfly begins as a caterpillar but is transformed in the cocoon, the Bride will be transformed as she allows her love for Christ to lead her through wilderness paths. May we always be willing to be changed because of our love for Jesus!

But we all, with open face beholding as in a glass the glory of the Lord, are changed into the same image from glory to glory, even as by the Spirit of the Lord (2 Corinthians 3:18).

Our Savior's invitation is to come and die; die to the flesh, die to self, die to the soulish powers of life and die to the old Adamic nature. This death is not an end. In reality, it is really a glorious beginning! After death comes resurrection life. After shedding the fleshly form of the caterpillar, the glorious butterfly emerges. What then will be the form of those children of God who allow the same process to work in them? We may see and appear like a lowly worm, but it is all because of perspective. We may feel and see low but we are now looking to the heights that God has prepared for us. We must set our affections on things above and not on things of the earth (see Colossians 3:2).

How is the Bride preparing?

Those who are proclaiming to be the Bride of Christ must see themselves in the same way that the King sees them. The King of Kings does not choose His Bride off the streets. He does not choose some worldly woman who has known every man who has come her way. These women are known as harlots and the King will not be defiled by harlotry. When the Bible speaks of harlotry, it speaks of spiritual harlotry. Many times God uses a harlot to describe His people.

When the King chooses a bride, or queen, she must always be a virgin. A virgin is one who has never given herself to any man. She is pure, holy, and untouched. Remember that God used a virgin to

We must set our affections on things above and not on things of the earth

conceive His Son, Jesus. The true Church is spoken of as being virgins. Spiritually speaking, the Bride of Christ will be made up of virgins. The virgin Church that our King chooses to be His queen will be chaste in every aspect of her life. She will be the most beautiful woman in His realm or sphere. Our God is looking for virgins who are the most desirable in all the earth.

Part of our preparation is learning the way God works in our lives. When we are seeking Him, He will lovingly allow adverse circumstances to arise and show us what is really in our hearts. There are times we do not like what we see. We must learn that the things going on around us are mere reflections of the realities that lie buried in our hearts unknown to us. We have a tendency to blame others for our predicaments when all along God is just trying to show us our own heart. He is trying to prepare us for something far greater than we could ever imagine.

Preparing as a Bride for the Coming Wedding

It's amazing that the Bible begins and ends with a marriage! The next major thing He did after the creation, is to institute marriage and one of the last major things that will happen, is the marriage of the Lamb! I believe that will help us as we try understanding God's heart toward a Bride. If we are so excited and looking forward to our wedding day here on earth, God is more excited about that day when, as the Bride of Christ, we will meet Him and be with Him forever! The Bible says that, as a bridegroom rejoices over his Bride, so our God rejoices over us.

For as a young man marrieth a virgin, so shall thy sons marry thee: and as the bridegroom rejoiceth over the bride, so shall thy God rejoice over thee (Isaiah 62:5).

But before that glorious day comes, I believe that the Church, corporately, should prepare as the Bride of Christ. There will come a day that the wedding of the Lamb will come and the Bride has made herself ready. That preparation must begin now and not later.

Jesus loves His Church so much that He gave Himself up for her. We must be set apart for Him and we must realize how holiness is such an essential quality of the Bride of Christ. He will present her to Himself as a radiant Church, without spot or wrinkle, or any other blemish. In short, He is doing a lot of things in the Church today as part of the preparation for that special day! He is the One preparing the Church in regard to the Bride of Christ. We need to be careful how we live our lives until Jesus returns for us. I believe we need to live a life that honors and pleases God, and walk in holiness daily. And best of all, let's remain faithful to our Bridegroom as we wait for His return.

Separation of the Bride of Christ

Our leaders who have been given the responsibility of feeding, guarding, and watching over the flock are the "watchmen." Here we are reminded of what happened to the Bride in the Song of Solomon.

The watchmen that went about the city found me, they struck me, they wounded me; the keepers of the walls took away my veil from me (Song of Solomon 5:7).

In this warning to the Bride, the "watchmen" are the "Keepers of the Wall" – those that keep the "Walls of Salvation" among the people. They have been charged with keeping the spiritual well being of the Body of Christ. These verses are prophetic for most of the spiritual leaders of today. They are watchman in name, but not in deed. They are the "Shepherds" that do not feed the flock as described in Ezekiel 34.

These leaders "smote" the Bride, and took away her veil – a part of her Bridal apparel. They removed the teachings of truth that would allow her to become prepared as a Bride. She will be separated from them, if she is to truly find Him whom her soul really loves. We must remember that it says in 2 Corinthians 6:17: "Wherefore come out from among them, and be ye separate, saith the Lord, and touch not the unclean thing; and I will receive you." That applies to the Bride of Christ.

As a bridegroom rejoices over his bride, so our God rejoices over us

For as Eve was the bride of Adam—and at the same time she was "of his bone and of his flesh"—so, we are the Bride of Christ, yet joined to Him in one Body. The Bride is being shaped and molded by the very hand of God. Even now, the Bride is being prepared to be the Bride of the last Adam. Much like Esther, who went through the 12 months of prescribed preparation before being brought into the presence of the King, so now the Messiah's Bride is being prepared to come into the presence of the King of Kings.

The Relation to Jewish Wedding Customs

There are crucial comparisons between the Jewish marriage customs, as they were practiced in the time of Jesus Christ. The time elements involved in the return of our Lord and Saviour which, if analyzed and properly understood, will support a more accurate interpretation of Scripture pertaining to His return. Let us first examine these customs related to the Jewish marriage ceremony and then compare these customs to scriptural references concerning Christ's return. We must remember that Jesus was a Jewish rabbi and He would know these customs.

The commentary in regard to the ancient Hebrew betrothal and wedding customs and how they relate to the Bride of Christ are very important. Let us examine some of those customs.

The Betrothal

The Jewish marriage is very similar to most other cultures and it begins with the betrothal. Marriage is, according to the Jews, a very formal ritual as well as a very sacred one. In Jewish marriage customs, the betrothal occurred when the man took the initiative, left his father's home and went to the home of the prospective bride to negotiate the purchase price. The bridegroom would negotiate with his prospective father-in-law, the purchase price of his bride. This price, referred to as the "mohar," had to be paid prior to any other events relating to the marriage. Once the price was paid, the marriage covenant was established and the man and woman were, for all intents and purposes, considered to be husband and wife at that point. The full definition of covenant, this ketubah marriage contract was only one small part of God's betrothal and marriage covenant with His bride. From that moment on, the bride was declared, "consecrated" or "sanctified" and was set apart exclusively for her bridegroom. When the price was agreed upon, there was a blowing of the shofar to announce the betrothal. This was a very important step in the process – from the price of the mohar to the blowing of the shofar!

The young man who wished to marry, back in ancient Israel times, would prepare a contract or covenant to present to the young woman and her father. This contract was his willingness to provide for her and described the terms under which he would propose marriage. One of the most important parts of the covenant or contract was the price the young man was willing to pay for the bride. This price was to be paid to the young woman's father in exchange for his permission to marry. In comparison, Jesus left heaven, His Father's house, and came to earth, the home of His bride, to pay the price for a lost humanity. Jesus, in the new covenant, paid the price for us, His Bride. His covenant provides forgiveness of our sins. The "mohar" was His life's blood. His blood now redeems us. Ephesians 1:7 states, "In whom we have redemption through his blood, the forgiveness of sins, according to the riches of his grace." Peter also stated this in his epistle:

> *Jesus left heaven, His Father's house, and came to earth, the home of His bride, to pay the price for a lost humanity*

Since you know that you were not redeemed with corruptible things, as silver and gold, from your vain manner of life received by tradition from your fathers; But with the precious blood of Christ, as of a lamb without blemish and without spot. (1 Peter 1:18-19).

The bridegroom's father chooses the bride; the groom in most cases does not. He sends a friend or a trusted servant to present the contract and come to terms with the parents of the prospective Bride, and make all the arrangements. We learned about that when Abraham sent his servant Eliezer after a bride for Isaac. The bride may not have any idea of what this person looks like or even know his age. All she knows is that she will spend her whole life with him if she says yes to this proposal!

This representative can be seen as a portrait of the Father and the Holy Spirit in the Scriptures. It is the Holy Spirit who nudges our hearts, and calls us to enter into this union with our Bridegroom Messiah. God determined that price beforehand. The groom obtained his bride through the establishment of a marriage covenant. In the same manner, Jesus came to the earth to establish a covenant. This covenant, foretold in the Old Testament by the prophet Jeremiah, was established the same night He gave the promise to His disciples. It is the New Covenant established by the shedding of His blood on the cross.

If the contract and price were completely satisfying to the young woman's father, the young man would pour a glass of wine for her. If she drank the wine, it would indicate that she accepted the proposal. The betrothal was legally binding, just like marriage. The only difference was that the marriage was not yet consummated. As a symbol of this covenant relationship that had been established, the groom and bride would drink from a cup of wine over which a betrothal benediction had been pronounced.

In the Jewish ceremony a shared cup of wine served as a symbol of the marriage covenant. In the Church today, the communion cup is the symbol of the covenant established by Jesus to obtain His Bride. Just as the bridegroom would pour a cup of wine to seal the marriage contract, so Jesus poured wine for His disciples. As believers, we must remember who we are and whose we are as we partake of this symbol of the covenant between our Bridegroom and us.

When the price had been paid, the Jewish bride was considered sanctified and set apart exclusively for her husband. The Church, too, has been declared sanctified, set apart exclusively for Jesus. In Ephesians 5:25-26, Paul teaches, "Husbands love your wives even as Christ loved the Church, and gave Himself for it; that He might sanctify and cleanse it with the washing of water by the word."

The author of Hebrews states that "We are sanctified through the offering of the body of Jesus Christ once for all (Hebrews 10:10). As the Bride of Christ, we recognize the truth of this verse.

The Preparation

Once the marriage covenant had been established, the groom would leave the home of his bride and return to his father's house. (It would be beneficial to note that many couples today do not realize that marriage is a covenant, or there wouldn't be as many divorces.) The groom would remain separated from his bride for an indefinite period of time—sometimes as long as a year or two.

During this time, both the groom and the bride had specific preparations that had to be accomplished prior to the wedding ceremony. The groom was required to prepare living accommodations for him and his new bride. This customarily involved building an addition to his father's house large enough for the two of them to live. Strong family ties were natural in the Jewish culture of Christ's day, normally precluded the building of a separate house away from the family. The groom's preparations would include not only the structure, but also everything needed to set up their new household. He would provide all that he could afford, in order to offer his bride the most comfortable and pleasant living accommodations possible. The bride, in anticipation of her married life, would busy herself with her trousseau and all her personal arrangements. Traditionally, during this separation, her mother would teach her all the things necessary to fulfill her marital responsibilities. It was a time spent in close fellowship, as both recognized their new roles in this relationship with each other.

We also see that Jesus, after paying the price, also departed to His Father's house to make preparation for His Bride. The promise of His return (John 14) includes His preparation on our behalf when He said, "I go to prepare a place for you." As the Jewish groom remained separated from his bride for an indefinite period of time, we see Christ's separation is also for an indefinite period of time. The Bride of Christ is now living in this period of separation. Just as the Jewish groom prepared living accommodations for his new bride in his father's house, Jesus is preparing accommodations for

117

us in His Father's house in heaven. Jesus will even take care of this for His Bride, for when He comes we will exchange our corruptible for the incorruptible. This should be a time when we would benefit in knowing more about our Bridegroom.

The Return for the Bride

After all the necessary preparations had been made, the Jewish groom returned for his bride to take her to be with him in their new home. The taking of the bride occurred at night and the groom would make his presence known by a shout. Christ will return for His Bride in like manner. It will undoubtedly be at night for some and day for others, as Paul tells us it will occur in the twinkling of an eye. We are now waiting for the blowing of the shofar to announce the wedding of the Lamb.

> For the Lord himself shall descend from heaven with a shout, with the voice of the archangel, and with the trump of God: and the dead in Christ shall rise first: Then we who are alive and remain shall be caught up together with them in the clouds, to meet the Lord in the air: and so shall we ever be with the Lord (1 Thessalonians 4:16-17).

With the coming and taking of the bride usually occurring at night, we see that the groom and his friends would form a procession and with lighted torches, they would proceed through the town so that all the townspeople would be aware of the wedding. Then, they would proceed to the home of the unsuspecting bride. The bride, even though anticipating the return of her groom, would never know exactly when he was coming for her. Therefore, she had to be constantly prepared for his return.

The procession would procede in silence, before arriving at the home of the bride, in order to surprise her. It was at this time that the groom would announce his return with a shout. The bride would then send a servant or a member of her household to get her bridesmaids and they would prepare for the journey to the home of the groom where the rest of the festivities took place. The bride would then gather her necessary belongings and join the procession through the town to her new home prepared by her husband. She would be wearing her wedding gown and her face would be veiled. The wedding guests would already be in attendance when the bridal pair arrived. Presumably, these guests had heard the procession and went straight to the house to help prepare for the wedding feast.

When the Jewish bride and groom returned to the father's house, the wedding guests had already congregated there in preparation for the feast. Similarly, when we get to heaven with Jesus, the wedding guests will already be there. We will find the souls of the Old Testament saints there, as guests, to celebrate with us.

The Consummation of the Marriage

When the groom came to take his bride to his father's house she went veiled, for it would have been considered improper for her face to be seen in public. The Jewish bride remained veiled until she was in the *huppah* (the bridal chamber). In like manner, the Church during this age does not know exactly who the other members of the Church are; as Paul says, "We see through a glass darkly." When Christ takes us to heaven though, we shall see each other as face-to-face.

When the bride and groom entered into physical union for the first time, they consummated the marriage and thereby completed the marriage covenant. Similarly, when the Church is taken to the Father's house in heaven we will enter into spiritual union with Christ thereby consummating the relationship that Christ covenanted with the Church over 2000 years ago.

Shortly after their arrival, their closest friends escorted the bridal couple to the bridal chamber, referred to as the "huppah." These friends, making up the wedding party, would then wait at the door while the couple consummated the marriage. This would finalize the marital agreement that had been made by them in a covenant earlier.

After the consummation, the groom would step out and announce to the wedding party that the marriage had been finalized and completed. (In later years it became tradition for the groom to bring out the sheet from off of the wedding bed to prove the chastity and virginity of his bride. This was a sign of honor to both him and his new wife.)

> *The Bride of Christ will be those who have an intimate relationship with Jesus in order to be that Bride*

Similarly, when the Bride of Christ is taken to the Father's house in heaven, we will enter into spiritual union with Christ. This will be the consummation of the relationship, which Christ made covenant with the Church over 2000 years ago. The author wishes to interject the thought, if some think the Church is the Bride—we will see that as in a physical wedding, the groom is not intimate with the whole wedding party. He is only intimate with his wife or his bride and the rest are just there as a part of the wedding feast after the wedding is consummated.

There is a strong belief in my heart that the Bride of Christ will be those who have an intimate relationship with Jesus in order to be that Bride. Again, only certain particular ones will be the Bride of Christ even though all will be in heaven. The truth is that not many people are willing to pay the price in order to walk in this higher covenant with God because "many are called but few are chosen." In other words, everyone is invited to the wedding festivities, and part of the wedding party, but there is only one that is the bride. She is the one that was chosen to be only for him. We also can be chosen to be the bride, and not just part of the marriage supper of the Lamb.

The Wedding Feast and the Seven Days of the Huppah

In the traditional Jewish marriage ceremony the marriage was consummated and the announcement was made to the wedding guests. This announcement would signal the beginning of the wedding feast. This feast would last seven days and during this time, their friends waited on the bride and groom, serving all their meals in the bridal chamber. Upon completion of the week, they would emerge from the bridal chamber and the bride would now be unveiled for all to see.

Just as the Jewish bride remained hidden in the huppah for a period of seven days, so will the Church remain hidden for a period of seven years. Both Daniel, in the Old Testament, and Revelation, in the New Testament, give the exact amount of time for this period. This is the period referred to in Revelation as "the tribulation." At the close of the wedding feast, the groom would proudly escort his bride out of the bridal chamber. She would now be unveiled for all to see, in full view. So, Christ will bring the Church out of heaven at the end of the Tribulation period in full view of all who are left alive. Paul told the Colossians of this event:

> For ye are dead, and your life is hid with Christ in God. When Christ, who is our life, shall appear, then shall ye also appear with him in glory (Colossians 3:3-4).

The Comparison

The promise of John 14:13: "And whatsoever ye shall ask in my name, that will I do, that the Father may be glorified in the Son" was given by Christ to His disciples in the Upper Room discourse. They did not immediately understand the passage, which is clear from Thomas' question, "Lord we know not whither thou goest; and how can we know the way?" (John 14:5). However, in this same discourse, Jesus tells His disciples He will send them the Holy Spirit, who will teach them all things and bring to their remembrance what

He had said. Later, through the ministry of the Holy Spirit, the disciples understood the promise in its proper context.

As Christians today, we do not understand the concept of Christ, the Bridegroom as the disciples understood it because we superimpose our own cultural customs of marriage on this promise and miss much of its significance. The idea that God's relationship to man is similar to the relationship of husband and wife has been taught extensively in the Old Testament.

Jesus, in the parable of the ten virgins, likened His relationship to the Church as the Bridegroom coming for the Bride. In answer to the Pharisee's question, "Why do the disciples of John fast often, and make prayers, and likewise the disciples of the Pharisees; but thine eat and drink?" Jesus refers to Himself as the Bridegroom saying, "Can ye make the children of the bride-chamber fast, while the bridegroom is with them?" (Luke 5:34).

We can compare marriage customs also with what the Bible has recorded about the return of Jesus Christ.

The Significance

The correlation between the Jewish marriage customs and the relationship Christ has with the Church is beautiful and full of significance to the believer and non-believer alike. First, to the believer, this relationship is significant for several reasons. It shows the believer the sequence of events that have led up to the present time of separation between the Church and Jesus Christ. It gives the believer hope for the return of Jesus and the re-establishment of the close personal relationship we will share with Him throughout eternity. It is significant in what it teaches about our present relationship to the risen Christ. In the Jewish analogy, it was possible for the Jewish bride to commit adultery. In the absence of her husband to be. She could do this by giving herself to another man. Even though the actual wedding ceremony had not yet taken place, this was still considered adultery. Today, it is possible for the believer to commit spiritual adultery in the absence of Christ. Paul expressed his concern over this issue when He wrote to the Corinthians and said:

> For I am jealous for you with a godly jealousy; for I betrothed you to one husband, that to Christ I might present you as a pure virgin. But I am afraid, lest as the Serpent deceived Eve by his craftiness, your minds should be led astray from the simplicity and purity of devotion to Christ" (2 Corinthians 11:23).

James was concerned about the same thing when he wrote that friendship with the world is hostility toward God. The context here seems to indicate that one commits spiritual adultery when he becomes more devoted to the godless world system than to Jesus Christ. The significance is to be applied personally; evaluate your relationship to the risen Lord to determine what it is He would have you to do in His absence.

Determine if He remains the center of your life and if you are eagerly awaiting His return. Ask yourself if He is controlling your every desire and thought? Also check to see if your relationship to the world is of more importance than Jesus. If you have been unfaithful in your relationship to Him, you can be confident He will forgive you, if you ask for His forgiveness.

2 Timothy 2:16 affirms His faithfulness toward us despite our actions. If we earnestly seek a closer walk with Him and desire Him to rule in our lives, we will readily admit our failure to remain pure. But upon confession we can be assured the Holy Spirit will renew our devotion and we can wait for His return confidently. Secondly, to the unbeliever, if you have never trusted Jesus Christ as your personal Savior, you have absolutely no part in the preceding analogy. If you do not establish a relationship with Jesus, you cannot become a part of His Bride or the Church.

Jesus Christ died on the cross for your sins; by His shed blood on that cross He paid the price for your sins. You can enter into this relationship by admitting your need for a Savior and by accepting Him. Just as the proposal of the Jewish bridegroom could be either accepted or rejected, you too can either reject or accept the offer that Christ makes to you each time you hear the gospel. The warning is this: if you continue to reject Him, He will reject you and you will spend eternity separated from God and Christ.

His very life will consume our daily life, moment by moment, as we are learning to walk beside Him as His Bride

If you accept Christ's proposal, your sins will be forgiven and you will enter into the relationship and can be a part of His Bride. You will be gathered together with Him when He returns. Accepting His plan of salvation is really quite simple. You simply believe that Jesus Christ is the Son of God, He came to earth and died to pay the price for your sins, and that He arose from the dead as proof that His sacrifice on your behalf was acceptable to God.

Learning to walk as the Bride

As we become increasingly aware that we are the Bride of Christ, we will be ever mindful of His heart and what He desires as we go about our daily lives. Only when we allow Him to be involved in every aspect of our lives can He then live through us. We are discovering that this relationship with Him is very real and is not limited to a few hours on Sunday morning or during our times of morning devotions. His very life will consume our daily life, moment by moment, as we are learning to walk beside Him as His Bride.

An important Scripture to remember in our walk with the Lord is:

And now, Israel, what doth the LORD thy God require of thee, but to fear the LORD thy God, to walk in all his ways, and to love him, and to serve the LORD thy God with all thy heart and with all thy soul (Deuteronomy 10:12).

For some people life seems to be a burden, an endless series of tasks that have no importance. There are difficulties in this earthly life, but to the Christian, we will find that life is filled with a purpose and power. We must be a changed people. When we accept Christ, He does a work in us.

In studying the first chapters of Acts, we see that this happened with the Apostles when they were filled with The Spirit of God. We must be a living witness to our risen Saviour. Each day we must walk as if today is our last day. We must be His witness every moment. Others are watching what we do, say, and teach. If they see in us the truth of what the Bible teaches, they will have a conviction in their heart.

There are parts of our lives that distract from our walk but each of us must look at his own life and ask the Lord to show us where we are not walking in His image. Our walk with the Lord must exemplify our talk.

Part of the process of being prepared as a Bride is purification. The whole purpose of preparation is to bring the Body to the place of being able to carry the glory of God in ways that we have not seen or experienced before. This preparation has to do with having our eyes opened to those things that we thought were of God but truly were the ways of tradition and religiosity. These ways of tradition tend to limit what God desires to do and actually separate us further from Him. Our hearts must be ready and willing to be examined before the Lord. Only those who desire truth are able to see the true condition of their hearts. That means we must maintain a continual place of humility and repentance.

The servants of God, who are hearing what the Spirit is saying, are declaring a living Word in the earth. It is this living Word that is preparing His people to receive Him. His living Word, is that which makes us ready as His Bride!

That is why He speaks very explicitly to the hearts of His people in the day and hour when He arises in the earth to do a new thing. It is not something that His servants have imagined out of their own hearts. It is something that originates in the heart of God.

It is His intention and His desire to bring it into being, and therefore He declares it. He speaks it forth. He knows that His Word is creative in its working, and nothing that He says can fail to come to pass, and so He speaks it forth. "For with God nothing shall be impossible" (Luke 1:37). This is what the angel said to Mary concerning the birth of her Son – something that was totally impossible as far as she could understand. And so He told her, and I believe this is a more literal translation: "No Word of God shall be void of power."

God, we pray, so deal with us in this hour that we will be concerned, like Mary of Bethany, or like David the shepherd of Israel, with only one thing; for "one thing is needful," and that is that we might sit at the feet of Jesus and hear what He has to say to our inquiring hearts. God is ushering His Bride into a time of being prepared and adorned. His desire is that she carry His glory and walk in a place of purity and power even now upon the earth. When we as the Church walk with the glory of the Father upon us, His Kingdom will be done on earth as it is in Heaven.

PREPARE FOR YOUR BRIDEGROOM
By Sharon Boaz

Come forth my people, come forth in triumph.

Your Bridegroom is at hand.

The time you have been waiting for is nigh – even at the door.

Prepare yourselves for the One whom you have long awaited.

Our Wedding Chamber is complete, the invitations has been sent.

I await My love, My beautiful Bride.

I long for the time when we will be as one.

Complete your preparation – watch and wait.

Listen for My voice. The banquet is set – Now all that is left

is for My Father to say,

"Go get Your Bride".

Await My love, await.

I will come and receive you to Myself.

I long for our appointed time.

Listen for the Final Shofar!

I am coming back for you!

Await My Bride, await.[4]

---

4 Sharon Boaz, *Prepare For Your Bridegroom,* http://www.mayimhayim.org

CHAPTER

7

BRIDAL LOVE ~ CONSUMED BY HIS PRESENCE

What is Bridal Love?

Obedience is always a key component in the Bridal love relationship with the Lord. Adam and Eve probably did not have the presence of the triune God in their hearts. They had God with them but not God within them or they would not have disobeyed God. It is not much different like a lot of people in our churches today – they know about God, but they do not know Him in an intimate relationship.

> Jesus answered and said unto him, "If a man love me, he will keep my words: and my Father will love him, and we will come unto him, and make our abode with him" (John 14:23).

May we allow the Lord to show us our heart and expose what is really inside our heart? What would you rather have: a perfect environment on the outside or a perfect God in the inside? God wants us to be transparent before Him at all times. God saw the heart of Adam and Eve and through disobedience, they were driven out of their perfect environment.

Once the Holy Spirit was poured out, God would have a new paradise that would far "outshine" the old one in Genesis. The Father, Son and Holy Spirit would come to dwell in the heart of man if only we would just obey Jesus. It does not seem like it would be too hard of a task, but it is. We must remember that Adam lost paradise through disobedience—the Christian may try to get it back through obedience, but that is not the solution. The paradise of God's Presence has by far a greater glory than the most beautiful landscape without weeds.

To receive and keep the residence of the Father, Son and Holy Spirit in our hearts, we must keep the weeds out of our hearts and have such love that we will obey God in everything and do whatever is pleasing to Him. We must not let our hearts be consumed by anything other than the Bridal love that Jesus has to offer us. The world and/or Satan is doing its best to keep us side-tracked and missing God's best for each of us every day. We have to keep our eyes on our goal and to make His love our aim in all we do in the world and in the Church.

There are various kinds of love, or perhaps, different levels or degrees of love. There is a difference between Redeeming Love, or the love of sinners, by which "God so loved the world, that he gave..." (John 3:16); and Shepherd's Love by which Jesus loves His sheep back into the sheepfold once it has been lost. And then there is the love that Jesus has for His obedient children that draws His very presence into their hearts—Bridal Love. This Bridal Love is best portrayed and represented in the Song of Solomon, which begins with these words: "Let him kiss me with the kisses of his mouth: for thy love is better than wine (Song of Solomon 1:2).

With this fervent, passionate love of the bride toward the bridegroom, she could then say, "He brought me to the banqueting house, and his banner over me was love" (Song of Solomon 2:4). Read the rest of the Song of Solomon and (with a little blushing) read about an intimacy that has no place anywhere else but in a

Bridal Love relationship. So, you see that John 14:23 is the New Testament connection to the Song of Solomon. It is Jesus singing the Song of Solomon—the most beautiful love song of the whole Bible to each one of us. It truly is a Bridal love. It is wonderful to experience and we can do that now and not wait till eternity. It is a relationship that grows deeper as we know Jesus in a more intimate way throughout our life.

Jesus could have said, "And if you want to know what this intimacy of love I speak of is all about, go read the Song of Solomon because that is exactly why I have placed it into the Bible." In other words, if you do not have red-hot, passionate love in your marriage, and if you did not have that stirring in your heart during courtship, then read what it's all about in the Song of Solomon. You can be single and/or alone and still enjoy this intimacy with the Lord. We must remember that relationship ought to be the romance between you and your Lord.

All loves are not the same. Most men have a love for their wife that they have for no one else. Most of us have a love for sinners that is different than our love for our spouse. There is a love for the back-sliders, but it is different than the love for a spouse and for sinners. There is also a love for my Lord and it is entirely different as well. Who do you want to be with almost all the time? Think about this question in regard to your affections and if it is the Lord and you desire to just be in His presence and spend time with Him, *this*, my friend, is Bridal Love.

> Jesus answered and said unto him, "If a man love me, he will keep my words: and my Father will love him, and we will come unto him, and make our abode with him" (John 14:23).

Is it possible to have the Holy Trinity live within us, if our love does not bring forth the fruit of obedience? If our love to Jesus is like that of the woman who anointed Jesus for His burial, He will also say to us, "She has done a beautiful thing to me ... She did what she could" (Mark 14:6-8 NIV). Has it ever occurred to you that just as Jesus can anoint you, so you can anoint Him and make His heart merry? Indeed, as we can grieve God's heart, we can also bring joy, comfort, and consolation to Him. We must reflect on this expression and facet of Bridal Love.

The way you become an anointer of Jesus, a comforter of Jesus, is to choose each moment of the day to do that which is pleasing in His sight. Don't look for the big things. It is faithfulness in the little things on a continuous basis that rejoices the heart of your Lover and causes Him to embrace you in the Spirit. Most often it is those small things that add up to be big blessings in our lives. A book that really reflects and reverberates this aspect of Bridal Love is by Basilea Schlink in her book, *My All for Him*. Here are some of those reflections.

"I bring joy and comfort to my Bridegroom Jesus when I can say in suffering, 'I want to bear this suffering out of love and gratitude to You.'"

"When plagued with fear, I declare, 'I trust You. You have conquered my fear.'"

"When following a difficult leading, I say, 'I know that You will make the bitter sweet.'"

"When I declare on paths of chastening, 'Thank You, Jesus. You are my heavenly Bridegroom. In Your love, You want to bless me through chastening and prepare me for the heavenly glory.'"[5]

Again, when we respond in such ways, we anoint the Lord Jesus and make His heart merry. Oh, my friend, will you become an anointer of Jesus? Will you give Him much joy in delighting in Him and His Presence? Will you allow Him to shower Bridal Love upon you?

5 Basilea Schlink *My All For Him*, (Bethany Publishing, June 1971)

Again, when we respond in such ways, we anoint the Lord Jesus and make His heart merry. Oh, my friend, will you become an anointer of Jesus? Will you give Him much joy in delighting in Him and His Presence? Will you allow Him to shower Bridal Love upon you?

> *The paradise of God's Presence has by far a greater glory than the most beautiful landscape without weeds*

So, Bridal Love is what it is all about, is it not? Consider Jesus' message to the seven churches as recorded in Revelation. The main point of Jesus' first message is love, and so is the main point of Jesus' last message to the churches. To the first church (at Ephesus) Jesus basically says: You have done a lot of good church work. I commend you for it, but "... I have somewhat against thee, because thou hast left thy first love. Remember therefore from whence thou art fallen, and repent, and do the first works; or else I will come unto thee quickly, and will remove thy candlestick out of his place, except thou repent" (see Revelation 2:4-5).

Do you see the picture the Lord is trying to portray for us? Is it not so that generally the time a couple loves each other the most fervently is when they first fall in love? Friends, we are supposed to keep that love ever before us and allow it to remain fresh—that first love. This is the love all true converts have toward Jesus on the day of their conversion. Jesus said to the Ephesian church: "You have lost that love, and if you don't repent, if you don't get it back, I will withdraw My life, My presence from you. Please return to your first love now. Be excited about your Bridal Love relationship."

If we no longer do everything to please Jesus, we have lost our first love, and we have lost the inner presence of the triune God.

Look again at John 14:23. This verse cannot be over-emphasized as part of being the Bride of Christ.

> Jesus answered and said unto him, "If a man love me, he will keep my words: and my Father will love him, and we will come unto him, and make our abode with him."

You may be saying, "I still feel the Lord's presence even though I know I'm not right in every way with God." Yes, you do feel His presence, but you are now in the Shepherd's Love and not in Bridal Love. You feel the Shepherd's love and care but it is not the same. Jesus calls you to come to complete obedience to get back into Bridal Love, to get back to the kissing and embracing of your Lover. Jesus desires our intimacy with Him and Him alone and that comes through our times of praise and worship.

So, in Jesus' seventh message to the churches, we see Him standing on the outside of the human heart. He wants us to open our heart but He sees that it is a heart that is not entirely surrendered to God. Yes, He is there at the door. He is there and you sense His presence. But He is on the wrong side of the door.

> Behold, I stand at the door, and knock: if any man hears my voice, and opens the door, I will come in to him, and will eat with him, and he with me (Revelation 3:20).

And so we see Him outside the door waiting for Christians that are not entirely obedient to open the door. In the famous painting of Jesus standing at the door knocking, you will see that there is not a latch on the outside; it can only be opened from the inside—by you. He is knocking at your door to come in. He desires to have fellowship with you. And once He is back in your heart—in Bridal Love with you—the only way you can keep Him there is by overcoming the self-life that tries to draw you away from His love. But if you continue to overcome the desires of the flesh—the Self—the day will come when you shall sit with Jesus in His throne, even as Jesus will sit in His Father's throne. Jesus desires each of us to have the life of an overcomer. In order for us to come over later, we must be that overcomer now!

The Bride of Christ will be a Bride that has become an overcomer. Some born-again Christians are daily being enriched with an ongoing, personal relationship with a loving Lord and they are over-comers even in this life now. Yet, there are many who are not overcomers; they are just plain and simply overcome by the circumstances of their life. To be an overcomer you must have that loving and intimate relationship with the Lord. It is His love that motivates us into service and ministry and it is through that love that we are ready and waiting for our soon coming Bridegroom.

The Holy Spirit was sent to provide us with that transforming power to become an overcomer. The Bride of Christ has a zeal for fruitful Christian service that is based upon her love relationship with her faithful Lord. Is it any wonder that the love chapter of 1 Corinthians 13 is between Chapter 12, which is the use of the spiritual gifts, and Chapter 14, which deals with prophecy? Love should be the center of all we do.

Our Christian life should be primarily a living, loving and spiritual relationship with the Father, Son and Holy Spirit and His family by being in Christ, who is the functional Head over His Church body. A commitment of love is the central key in the love relationship between Christ and His Church. His overcoming Bride-to-be develops a true love toward the Lover of her soul and the way we endure is by being faithful to His Word. We must see the need to become more submissive to Jesus and His words as an important challenge to living an overcoming Christian life. An overcomer appreciates the Holy Spirit's power and Christ life influence over his or her life. An overcomer is ever mindful of the fact that Christ "loved the Church and gave Himself for her" (Ephesians 5:25). As a result, the complete Christ, the Bridegroom, is to be revealed to His Church.

To be a part of the Bride of Christ is to receive the highest honor. The Bride is given intimate access to the Bridegroom; the two will become one. This honor, however, is not given freely. It is reserved for those whose hearts beat with a passion for the Lord Jesus Christ. It is reserved for those who have allowed the work of the cross to bring a cleansing and separation in their lives, removing that which is fleshly. It is an intimate relationship with the Lord. We will experience that the Bride of Christ is a loving and beautiful Bride, an Overcoming Bride, and an Obedient Bride. There are five influential characteristics that are brought out in the Song of Solomon.

Five Important Principles From The Song of Solomon

The Lord revealed these principles to me out of this account of the Shulamite woman searching for her Beloved in the Song of Solomon:

1. She was yearning for the One she loved.

She was willing to be inconvenienced in the middle of the night to get out of bed to go search in pursuit of Him. She couldn't or wouldn't wait till morning to go find her Lover. She could not sleep in anticipation of finding her Beloved. The Lord is causing His Church to arise out of the bed of our comfort and complacency to search for our Beloved as well. We must proceed to get out of our comfort zone or complacency and be willing to look for Him even if it is at odd hours when the rest of the world is asleep.

2. She didn't find Him right away.

She had to continue to look and search for Him. She did not give up in discouragement, but kept on pursuing her Lover. The Lord is not always easily found and He may surprise us by showing up somewhere totally unexpected. Sometimes there has to be a persistent and consistent search for God until we find Him, even though we may not find Him immediately.

She did not want to ever give up on her search for Him and the search was continuously on-going until she reached her goal. Sometimes, we just quit too soon in our pursuit of something we want in our lives.

3. The watchmen couldn't tell her where He was.

There are those times where we need to find God for ourselves. We can't live off someone else's experience or anointing. We have to dig our own well and find the presence, power and anointing of God in our own lives. Other's testimonies can encourage us, but we must always press in to find God. We each must have our *own* personal encounter with the Lord.

When we find the Lord, we cannot be easily satisfied by anything else. We must not quit too soon and settle for second best—we must be **persistent** and **consistent** when we are actively seeking and pressing into God. There are times when others will show us the way and other times we are on our own.

4. When she finally found Him; she would not let Him go.

This is where we miss it. We must be like Jacob, who wrestled with the Angel of the Lord all night until He blessed him. He would not let the angel go and this is how we must be with the Lord. We must be relentless and not let Him go until we have the fullness of what He wants to bless us with. When Jacob wrestled with God, there was a name change from Jacob to Israel; but there was a bigger change than the name change—it was an internal change. He went from "Deceiver" to "Prince with God." This shows that there was a deep transformation that took place in Jacob. As we wrestle with God and refuse to let Him go until we have His full blessing and favor, there will also be a deep transformation in us as we become more like Him, being transformed into His image. What a transformation!

5. They entered the chamber of intimacy.

This is where new birth is conceived, in the secret place with God. It is in this chamber of deep intimate love with God that His seed of revival is imparted into us. It will be an experience like no other with the Lord.

These principles found in the Song of Solomon demonstrate our discipline, determination, devotion and delight when we find Jesus as our Bridegroom. We will find great comfort in following His leading in our lives. It is in the Song of Solomon that we see seeking is an important and vital part of that relationship of Bridal Love. It is like it says in Psalm 105:4 that says "Seek the LORD, and his strength: seek his face evermore."

Solomon in all his wisdom wrote the Song of Solomon, which is indeed a love song about a longing and loving relationship between two lovers. This is God's song to His Bride as well. It is confirmed that God sings over us:

The LORD thy God in the midst of thee is mighty; he will save, he will rejoice over thee with joy; he will rest in his love, he will joy over thee with singing (Zephaniah 3:17).

The Song of Solomon was not written with human understanding, but was written out of a heart filled with emotion that went beyond Solomon's human intellect. We cannot exhaust all the meaning of the symbolism that is found in this song. A lifetime will never deplete all the types and shadows that are depicted and portrayed no matter how much we study this book of the Song of Solomon.

CHAPTER

8

THE SECRET PLACE OF INTIMACY WITH THE LORD

This chapter is continuing about Bridal Love and it is all about the Secret Place with the Lord. The word "Intimate" is defined in Webster's 1828 Dictionary as: "A familiar friend or associate; one to whom the thoughts of another are entrusted without reserve."[6] The New Oxford Modern English Dictionary defines the word "intimate" as: "closely acquainted, familiar, close; private and personal; detailed, thorough; friendly; promoting close personal relationships; a very close friend."[7]

The Lord is a friend who we can share our deepest thoughts and our heart without reserve. Our heart is only enraptured for Him. It is mentioned in Song of Solomon 4:9a, "Thou has ravished my heart." "Ravished" is defined as: "to fill with strong emotion, especially joy."[8] So, when the Lord says that His heart is ravished for us it takes on a different connotation in that He is filled with the strong emotion of joy toward us.

---

6 Noah Webster, *Webster's 28th Dictionary*, http://www.cbtministries.org/resources/webster1828, s.v. "Intimate."
7 Ibid
8 Ibid

What Is Spiritual Intimacy?

There is so much being spoken today about a personal intimate relationship with God, not just in heaven someday, but here and now on earth. A distinction is being presented between knowing about God and intimately knowing Him.

The best way to describe this relationship comes through a friend that has written about this in regard to the Bride of Christ.

"To speak of an 'intimate relationship' with Christ means to know Him and to be known by Him deeply and completely. For the believer, it means there is no place within us that is held back from Him; no part of our lives where He is not Lord; no sin or fear that is not surrendered to Him. It means the knowledge of Christ is our greatest desire and consequently our greatest pursuit. Notice this is not knowledge about Christ; it is not accumulated information about His Word, His teachings or His life history. This is speaking of the deep experiential knowledge of Him gained only through sincerely seeking His face in worship and spending time in His Presence and His Word personally.

"The riches of Christ are so deep they will be continually unfolding to us throughout eternity, but we do not need to wait until we enter Heaven to begin to know Christ. We can know Him now in this realm. From the moment we are born again, the Holy Spirit begins revealing Christ to us. It is this knowledge of Him, or communion with Him, that we call intimacy.

"This spiritual intimacy can in some ways be compared in our understanding to the close physical intimacy and fellowship of a strong and healthy marriage relationship. However, the Scriptures are clear that the spiritual and the natural do not always mix. As Jesus explained to Nicodemus, that which is born of flesh is flesh, and that which is born of the Spirit is spirit (John 3:6). God is Spirit and those who worship Him must worship Him in spirit and in truth. Therefore, there should be no doubt or confusion that, when we are speaking of intimacy with God, we are speaking in terms of Spirit to spirit."[9]

Common Union or Communion

When God created mankind, it was for the purpose of fellowship and communion. Adam and Eve originally had the great privilege of walking with God the Creator in the cool of the day. This implies friendship, fellowship and intimate communion between God and mankind. They not only had a common union, but we must also keep in mind that it was God who came searching for this communion with Adam and Eve after they had sinned.

God has always been the initiator in seeking man's fellowship, friendship and above all, a relationship. God responded immediately when that original fellowship was broken through mankind's sin. God did not waste any time in establishing a plan for His restoration of this relationship.

> *Intimacy with Christ is the reward for those who are maturing into the Bride of Christ*

Intimacy with Christ is the reward for those who are maturing into the Bride of Christ. In the New Testament, the Apostle Paul obviously understood Christ's love for the Church in terms of a Bridegroom for His Bride. He wrote to the Corinthians "I have betrothed you to one husband, that I may present you as a chaste

9 Cheryl McGrath, *Bread for the Bride*, http://www.greatsouthland.org/, (October 2009)

virgin to Christ" (2 Corinthians 11:2); and he wrote to the Ephesians: "Husbands, love your wives, just as Christ also loved the Church and gave Himself for her ... For this reason a man shall leave his father and mother and be joined to his wife, and the two shall become one flesh. This is a great mystery, but I speak concerning Christ and the Church" (Ephesians 5:25, 30-32). John the Baptist referred to Jesus as a Bridegroom seeking His Bride (see John 3:28, 29) and Jesus also described Himself as a Bridegroom having come for His Bride (see Mark 2:19, 20).

> *After the information, comes the transformation that the Lord does in each of our lives and the result is the conformation*

Why does God choose to use the word "bride" to describe those who know Jesus and are known by Him? The complete answer to that mystery will only become evident in eternity. However, it may help to consider this: Is there any other relationship known among human beings worldwide that is more unique, deeply abiding, mysterious and universally understood, than the covenant union between a man and a woman, as it was originally ordained to be by our Creator? Could God have chosen any more revealing way to convey His desire for the covenant meal of communion and fellowship with us than the words "Bride" and "Bridegroom"? Marriage is just a contract, but when God enters into the marriage, it makes a covenant. Whether we admit it or not, marriage is a covenant with God and each other! God is a Covenant-keeping God.

But the mercy of the Lord is from everlasting to everlasting upon them that fear him, and his righteousness unto children's children; to such as keep his covenant, and to those that remember his commandments to do them (Psalm 103:17-18).

God understands and values covenant. He desperately desires covenant relationship with us. Unfortunately, in the Western church, we don't understand or honor covenant nearly as completely as He does. This matter of covenant is very important to God, because covenant is how God operates with His people. Whenever God decides to move to restore a right relationship with mankind, which we lost through sin, He does it by covenant. Covenant is much more than just a contract or legal document, because it is relationship based. Rather than a legalistic set of rules and regulations, true God ordained covenant is an organic growing process of interaction between God and mankind. When Christ returns to the earth, there will be a covenant-keeping Bride waiting for Him.

In a purely spiritual realm, God is captivated and enamored with the beauty of His Bride and greatly desires her. He greatly admires every feature of her spiritual being. He longs to shower her with the most beautiful and finest of gifts. Also, in a purely spiritual realm, fully redeemed mankind is overcome with adoration and a deep sense of pure spiritual worship for God. He is fully willing to lay aside all others and everything else to be close and become one in the Spirit with God. What a true picture of intimacy with the Lord.

Intimate communion with God in the spiritual realm will change who we are in the natural realm. Life and strength of well-being for one's soul and body comes through one's spirit from God through the Holy Spirit. We are spirit beings who live in a body and have a soul. The Holy Spirit transforms us into the character and nature of Christ. Only pure, holy righteousness can come together intimately with God. It is in Christ by the Holy Spirit that we become intimate with our Heavenly Father. Partial righteousness cannot intimately relate to a holy God. God gives us the information we need in order to have this intimate relationship with Him. After the information, comes the transformation that the Lord does in each of our lives and the result is the conformation. And as we are conformed to the image of Jesus individually, we can have that intimacy with God and enjoy its blessings now.

Seeking an intimate relationship with God is important

The process begins with coming into contact with the love of God at the cross of Christ Jesus, where His pure blood was shed to pay for our sin. Brokenness begins with realizing how much He loved us. He loved us enough to come from heaven and give His life in a painful, dishonorable death on the cross to provide the way for us to come to God. The power of His resurrection from the dead is available to cleanse and undo all the works of ungodliness in our spirit, soul, and body. The empowerment of His life is available through His return as a "life-giving Spirit"—the Holy Spirit—to indwell and produce the character and nature of His life in us. Our part is to fully appropriate the work of Jesus by faith, with a willingness to be conformed into that likeness of Jesus.

There are two major tools the enemy uses to cause people to miss the reality of full redemption unto holiness through fully appropriating the work of Christ Jesus. He uses religion and secularism to produce a replacement belief system that influences people toward unbelief and doubt in the words and ways of God. Other spirits are introduced through education and enticement that promote the pride of life and the lust of the flesh. This causes a closing of the spiritual senses and leaves only the natural human senses. Through this process, the intended relationship with God is replaced with religion and secularism. God does not want us to just have religion. He wants that individual relationship that only He can give to each of us.

The process of coming to God in intimate relationship involves seeking Him with our whole hearts. Some of you think "How can I seek God with my whole heart since it has been broken by so many other relationships, etc.?" We must learn how to give God all the pieces of our brokenness, so He can make it whole again. The hole in our hearts must be repaired and mended, so it will be whole again in order to seek Him with our whole heart. This will require growing in faith through changing the focus of our hearts and lives from the things of this world (including our secular and religious belief systems) through the Word of God, prayer, and relationship with holy people of God. This is repentance from dead works and turning from natural, fallen, human nature toward living an abundant spiritual life now.

Intimacy with God is a journey. It is a quest that requires a journey for the rest of our lives. Our quiet times with the Lord are absolutely essential for the development of our intimate relationship with God.

As we put aside these times of quiet (or sometimes noise), depending on how we spend that time, we are purposefully asking God to draw us into His close embrace and we are positioning ourselves to hear from Him and to share our deepest thoughts with Him, just as He shares His with us.

> *Intimacy with God is a journey. It is a quest that requires a journey for the rest of our lives*

Do you feel far from God— guess who moved?

Of course, we first need to understand that our quiet times are not simply going through our prayer lists or reading Scripture in a religious manner. These times with God can include prayer and Scripture reading, but the purpose must primarily be to connect with God and let Him connect with us. This may be reading Scripture, listening to Christian music and worshiping God; prayer of various kinds (petitions, intercessory, warfare etc.) or simply positioning ourselves before God in silence.

Be still and know that I am God (Psalm 46:10a).

It is important to say that our quiet times need to include times of silence before God. This is when we learn to hear God's voice and feel His heartbeat. It is also when we learn to pray according to what is on His heart and not simply what we feel we should be praying. Remember that we are called to be the Bride of Christ and He desires to have times of intimacy with us.

> A lawyer, asked Him a question, testing Him, and saying, "Teacher, which is the great commandment?" Jesus said to him, "You shall love the LORD your God with all your heart, with all your soul, and with all your mind. This is the first and great commandment" (Matthew 22:35-38).

> For the eyes of the LORD run to and fro throughout the whole earth, to show Himself strong on behalf of those whose heart is loyal to Him (2 Chronicles 16:9).

Jesus tells us what God is looking for—LOVE—intimate love. He is looking for love responses from our very heart. He is after our heart (not our talent, gifts or money). He desires spontaneous, intentional, wholehearted love from each one of us. It is brought about through the spirit of abandonment to God. He wants to take over our lives. God created us for a specific purpose and designed us with longings to fulfill that purpose in each of our lives.

He requires and expects that we love Him with all our heart and strength because He loves us that way. His glory is always the first reason for His actions in creation and redemption. However, we must remember that YOU are a significant reason. You are very much a part of this relationship as He pours His love on us and receives it back from us. He does it all for love. He freely gave us love, so we can freely give it back to Him.

One of the highest callings we have is to move God's heart with our love. Our highest purpose is to love God and Him alone. This comes ahead of seeking to make an impact or to be successful from man's point of view. Many of us want to build a big ministry for God, but He first wants and desires our love.

The basis of this truth is that God equips us to love Him and to know and feel His affection toward us. The Father feels the same intensity of love for us as He feels for Jesus. WOW! That should make us feel good. The Father has delighted in Jesus from all eternity. We are known as the apple of His eye.

Keep me as the apple of the eye, hide me under the shadow of thy wings (Psalm 17:7)

When we know the King loves us, we should be unmoved even when others overlook or mistreat us. We can see from that verse that God wants to protect us by hiding us under the shadow of His wing. He is our covering at all times.

The measure of the Father's love (affection) for His Son Jesus is the measure of His love for all His sons and daughters. This is the ultimate revelation of our worth. This truth gives us the right to stand before God with confidence as one of "His favorites."

They That Wait on The Lord

They that wait upon the Lord shall renew their strength; they shall mount up with wings as eagles; they shall run, and not be weary; and they shall walk and not faint (Isaiah 40:31).

Wait for the Lord and keep His way. He will exalt you to inherit the land (Psalm 37:34).

Do not leave Jerusalem but wait for the gift my Father promised, which you have heard me speak about (Acts 1:4).

When we wait on the Lord, it brings blessings (waiting usually precedes the blessing). But we need to ponder this thought and consider what it really means to "wait on the Lord!"

Waiting on the Lord is the period between when God gives you a promise and when the promise is realized. Abraham was promised a son when he was 75 years old; he was 100 years old when Isaac was born, waiting 25 years for the promised son. Moses knew he was to be the deliverer of the Israelites when he was 40 years old; he led the Israelites out of Egypt when he was 80 years old, waiting 40 years to carry out his purpose on earth. David waited about 25 years after he was anointed king by Prophet Samuel, before he actually sat on the throne as the king in Israel. These are examples of those whom have waited on the Lord.

Waiting on the Lord indicates there is already a promise in hand. It could be having a child, marrying a God-fearing spouse, waiting for breakthrough in that lousy marriage, starting a ministry, building a new church facility, hitting it big with that business idea, starting a church, or many other personal promises God has made to us that He wants to do for us as we learn to wait on Him.

Why do we have a time waiting on God?

As we study the lives of people God used to accomplish great purposes in the Bible, there is a pattern of promise, waiting and fulfillment. We will notice that while these men or women focus on the promise they have in hand and the fulfillment, God is more focused on the journey they take to their destination. God is always more concerned about our character and the relationship developed between Him and us that we build on this journey. We must learn to dwell on the promises of God and not on the problem.

An example of this process is found in Genesis 12:1-3, where God called Abram out of his father's house to journey with Him and gave him these seven promises.

[1] I will make you a great nation.

[2] I will bless you.

[3] I will make your name great.

[4] You will be a blessing.

[5] I will bless those who bless you.

[6] I will curse those who curse you.

[7] Peoples on earth will be blessed through you.

At the time of this promise, we must remember that Abram was 75 years old and his wife about 65 years old; they had no children, yet the promises of God to Abram hinged on having a child to carry this legacy on for them. It took another 25 years for the promise of a son to be fulfilled. In those 25 years, Abraham became so close to God that he was called a friend of God and it was after time that he even trusted God with the life of his son on Mount Moriah.

> *We must learn to dwell on the promises of God and not on the problem*

Joseph was 17 years old when he had his first dream about his family bowing to him. His dreams irritated his step-brothers, who wanted nothing to do with serving their baby brother. Also, things even got more complicated when their father, Jacob, showed extreme favoritism and preferential treatment to Joseph.

The brothers thought of killing Joseph when he brought them supplies in the field but, instead, they sold him off, thinking his dream of God's plan would never materialize because now he was a slave. He was sold into Potiphar's household where his master's wife was attracted to him; he was falsely accused and ended up in jail until he interpreted Pharaoh's dream. It took 13 years, from when Joseph had his first dream to when he became the prime-minister of Egypt, and another 7 years or more before his family bowed to him, as he had seen in his dreams. We must remember that Satan always tries to destroy or steal our dreams from us so we cannot reach the destiny the Lord has placed within us.

Joseph sure did learn that God's timing is better than anyone else's. His brothers had forgotten him in the pit and the king's butler had forgotten him in prison. In both cases, Joseph was elevated to a higher position. He learned not to hold a grudge because everything always works out for those who love God and are called according to His purpose. Twice he went from shame to fame—from being on a slave trading block, to being the head of Potiphar's household; and from prison, to being the prime-minister of Egypt. Joseph truly went from the pit to the palace and it was there he saw the hand of God helping him fulfill his God-given destiny.

We can look in the Bible for more stories of men who waited on the Lord. Moses waited 40 years after he knew he would be the deliverer. David waited about 25 years, after Samuel anointed him king, before he sat on the throne.

Remember that Moses learned a lot about humility and total reliance on God. He went from being an alumni of one of the best schools in the world, in Egypt, to being a shepherd on the backside of a desert in a foreign land and learning lessons from the school of hard knocks. Moses went from walking with kings and nobles and living in a palace, to being alone in the desert with dirty, smelly sheep. We find that Moses learned how to move from a mere relationship with the Lord into fellowship with Him. We discover that during those 40 years in tending sheep, Moses went from a place of preparation to purpose to passion in order to walk in fellowship, and all because of learning to wait on God's timing in his life.

Moses developed patience, something perhaps he lacked as a prince in Egypt because people waited on him, and now he would need to learn how to wait on God. We have to see the necessity of not only taking time to wait on God, but to wait on the timing of God. Both of these are vitally important and very different. Are you taking the time to wait on God for some area of your life and are you waiting on the timing of God?

David had just been successful in killing the giant, Goliath of Philistine, and was being pursued by his own king (Saul). While running from Saul, he was housed by the same Philistines whose giant he had killed (that is called *favor*—when you are housed and fed by your enemy). David demonstrated the mercies of God when he had the opportunity to kill King Saul twice, but did not do it. Subsequently, Godly protection was accorded to his men and himself as they moved from one place to another.

The lives of these men show a God that is particular about having more than a relationship with us and that He is interested in shaping us into His mold, building a strong character that will sustain us when we reach the promised land (the purpose He has for us). The lives of these men reveal refined people that learned to walk with God in the waiting period. There is nothing more fulfilling that having a close relationship and being called God's friend, in spite of worldly achievements or accolades.

What to do when waiting

In our world today, the waiting period is now very complicated with the desire to have material wealth and have it now. We live in a microwave society that wants many things instantly. Then there is the desire to be known and be popular. Or the instant gratification attitude provoked by expert marketing strategies and the use of credit cards, etc. What we are going through in our generation, however, does not change the principles of God or His processes of refining us for a relationship through waiting on Him.

Knowing the Word of God is very critical to your sustenance in the waiting period. The Bible says, "... and you will know the truth, (the truth you know) and it will set you free." As we are waiting on God, there will be other options brought on by the devil and even advice from friends (like what happened to Job), but when you know the truth (Christ Himself as the truth and His words as truth), you will be able to say no to advice that is contrary to the Word.

The gift of discernment is also crucial in the waiting period. Discernment comes as your relationship with the Lord grows; it comes from constant study, constant prayer and constant communion. Consistency and persistency is of utmost importance. Just as children learn to recognize their mom's voice in a crowd, as God's children, we must recognize His voice when He speaks to us. It is because of our relationship with each other that we are able to have this discernment.

Immerse and absorb yourself in the Bible and in prayer, memorize Scripture that pertains to your situations and remind your self of God's promise and remind Him of His words. God doesn't need to be reminded about your situation. Dwell on the promises of God and not your problems.

The Blessing of Waiting

It is in being persistent and consistent in our time of intimate relationship of waiting that we will find blessings. It is when you learn to wait on the Lord for His timing that His purpose is achieved in your life and your heritage on earth will last till He returns. Earlier we read about biblical men who learned to wait and in our contemporary times we read of godly men like Billy Graham, David Wilkerson, A.J Tozier, D.L. Moody, Smith Wigglesworth, the

Wesley Brothers, Martin Luther, etc. These ministries continue to have impact on lives years after many of them are deceased.

I don't know what it is that God has promised you as you read this book. I know that He who promised is able to fulfill that promise. His timing is not your timing. While you might be concerned about getting the promise, He desires a relationship with you as you journey to that purpose; so that when He exalts you and you inherit the land, you will direct the glory to Him and not toward yourself.

> *As God's children, we must recognize His voice when He speaks to us*

Romans 8:28-30 has always been one of my favorite sections of Scripture, because it assures me that whatever event I go through is under the hand of God. My circumstances may not seem like an instant blessing during the waiting, but it is part of a process and has a purpose.

> And we know that in all things God works for the good of those who love Him, who have been called according to His purpose. For those God foreknew he also predestined to be conformed to the image of his Son, that he might be the firstborn among many brothers and sisters. And those he predestined, he also called; those he called, he also justified; those he justified, he also glorified (Romans 8:28-30).

This passage of Scripture has many facets and we need to understand what these are and that the Lord will help make us shine for His glory. Part of these processes and purposes are seen in that verse in Romans 8: "… we know that in all things …" This is a word of assured confidence. Notice it does not say, "we hope" or "we wish" but rather, "we know." We really can know that we have this kind of assurance when our experiences have been so devastating. We know, not by looking at circumstances, but by knowing God and

His Word, that God is sovereign in every detail of our lives. This reminds us that we can acknowledge this truth no matter what we are going through in our life.

"... God works together for good ..." shows that God is at work and He is sovereign. God certainly knows what is good for us because He's a good God. God is not saying that all things are good, but that he works His ways and His will together to accomplish His good. With that in mind, even problems can be profitable and that is part of the purpose of Romans 8:28.

We might not always immediately understand the good that God is accomplishing, but He is working His will in a way that gives Him glory and brings us ultimate good. We will emphasize the importance of being called and what is God's purpose in all this.

> *God's good for us is not our comfortability, but our conformity to Christ*

The last part of verse 28 spells out that God has a purpose behind His plan. "... who have been called according to His purpose." What that really means is that there are no accidents in God's economy. God's ultimate purpose is not to save me, or to meet my needs. His ultimate purpose is to bring glory to Himself by conforming me to the image of His Son. We see that in the middle of verse 29: "... to be conformed to the likeness of His Son ..." and if God's glory is the goal, then His good for us is not our comfortability, but our conformity to Christ. That means He is more committed to our holiness than to our happiness. 2 Corinthians 3:18 says that He is making the saved like His Son: "And we, who with unveiled faces all reflect the Lord's glory, are being transformed into his likeness with ever-increasing glory, which comes from the Lord, who is the Spirit." Whatever you're wrestling with today, remember that God's plan is bigger than your problem. God has a promise in His Word for your situation.

In order to accomplish this purpose of bringing glory to Himself, God designed a process:

> For those God foreknew he also predestined to be conformed to the likeness of his Son, that he might be the firstborn among many brothers. And those he predestined, he also called; those he called, he also justified; those he justified, he also glorified (Romans 8:29-30).

This passage explains Romans 8:28 and is what makes it true. We see this in these five key words, like links in a chain. These parallel clauses are closely connected.

1. God chose us. This is the word "foreknew." Before you and I were even born, God knew us. Jeremiah 1:5 says: "Before I formed you in the womb I knew you, before you were born I set you apart ..."

2. God changes us. Foreknowledge determines who God's children will be; predestination determines what God's children will be. God is chipping away at us to conform us into the image of Christ, not to make us comfortable. Don't get hung up on the word "predestined."

3. God calls us. The next link in the chain is the word "call" which means "invited" and was originally used of those who received invitations to a banquet. God has given a general call to everyone and then a specific call to those who will respond. If you're a Christian, you're called; if you're not a Christian, then you need to respond to His call.

4. God cleanses us. In studying the word "justified" throughout the Book of Romans it essentially means "to declare righteous."

5. God completes us. The word "glorified" means to be clothed with the glory that God Himself has. This is still future but I want to point out that each of these words is in the past tense. That means that it is so certain that it's as if it happened already. God's purpose is to bring us all the way to glory.

God's purpose is all wrapped up in this process—and that's why we can believe the promise of Romans 8:28.

Defining Our Wholehearted Love for Jesus

You shall love the LORD your God with all your heart, with all your soul, with all your mind, and with all your strength. This is the first commandment (Mark 12:30).

It is vital to see the explanation of that verse and it will give us understanding of our wholehearted love relationship with Jesus.

1. Love with all our heart: with all our affection and that includes emotions. We change our mind and God changes our heart or emotions. Our emotions will follow whatever we set ourselves to pursue. We can set our heart and mind to be filled with zeal for God.

2. Love with all our soul: our personality is expressed in a dynamic way by our speech in what we say. We must determine to express our personality by speaking and acting in a way that enhances, not diminishes, love toward God and toward each other.

3. Love with all our mind: we fill our minds with long and loving meditation on God's Word. We should daily resist putting anything in our minds that diminishes love for Jesus and quenches the Holy Spirit in our intimate relationship with the Lord. We must fill our mind with edifying each other in the Lord.

4. Love with all our strength: with our resources (time, money, talents, reputation, and influence).

How do we really love God? All of God's commands bring with them the promise of His supernatural enabling to obey them. We must actively cultivate extravagant devotion to Jesus. We need to know that this takes time and effort on our part. Love does not automatically grow. Usually love diminishes unless we intentionally cultivate a responsive heart toward the Lord, or in our relationship with others. Every one of us must have a determination to make a purposeful decision to love God with all our heart, soul, mind and strength.

Our love is often expressed through our obedience. God chose for us to express our love to Him in a way that brings glory and honor to Him. We must remember that each of us has a different struggle and a different assignment from which we offer our gift of love to God.

We must see this revelation of God's love and how it equips our heart to love Jesus. We love God with all our heart only as we see that He loves us with all His heart. He empowers us by revealing His love to each one of us.

We gain revelation of God's love by mediating on it from God's Word. We have to position ourselves to receive from His heart by feeding on His Word. We will sit long hours before God in His Word because we are hungry to understand the affections of His heart. It often takes time to build that love relationship.

> For the word of God is living, and powerful, and sharper than any two-edged sword, piercing even to the dividing asunder of soul and spirit, and of the joints and marrow, and is a discerner of the thoughts and intents of the heart (Hebrews 4:12).

Jesus gives His secrets to those who desire them enough to sit for hours before Him. Many times we have to discipline ourselves to wait in His Presence until it becomes a delight to just to be in that relationship with Him.

> Delight thyself also in the LORD: and he shall give thee the desires of thine heart (Psalm 37:4).

> The secret of the LORD is with them that fear him; and he will show them his covenant (Psalm 25:14).

157

Let us consider how our relationships contribute to how we receive much of God's love in serving, sharing and receiving it from others. God's love is only seen in fullness when the whole Body functions together. Some of our inheritance and healing is in the hands of others who reveal and release God's love to us.

We must set our heart to love Jesus like we never have before. We must have a sustained vision to go deeper in God. It takes focus and effort to do this, or we will be easily swayed by every wind of doctrine. Our soul prospers as we grow in the anointing to love.

Satan's first priority against the Bride of Christ is to lead us astray from cultivating the ability to be responsive to God with wholehearted love and extravagant devotion. If Satan leads us astray from the purity of devotion to Jesus, then our service and love for others will eventually fail as well.

Sustaining a fresh walk with God is the definition of living radically before God. We are not radical because we do something unusual for a few weeks or months, but we make it a life-long desire and determination to have continual and intimate relationship with the Lord.

Remember that David sustained his passion for God for decades and was determined to do so *all* the days of his life.

One thing I ask from the LORD, this only do I seek: that I may dwell in the house of the LORD all the days of my life, to gaze on the beauty of the LORD and to seek him in his temple (Psalm 27:4).

The main source of teaching on intimacy in the Bible is contained in the book of Song of Solomon, which is a beautiful picture of not only King Solomon and a Shulamite woman, but also of Christ and His Bride. As we see in the Song of Solomon, Jesus is passionately and completely in love with His Bride and very often, during our quiet times or during times of high worship, He will express His love and passion for us through prophetic utterance.

As with the Shulamite woman in the Song of Solomon, we should be so taken up with our love for God that our words of love, passion, adoration and worship will rise to His throne room as sweet-smelling incense. We should be just consumed by His Presence. It is God's heart for us that we enter further and deeper into the Glory realm of God, both in our times of worship and intercession and also in our daily lives.

It is God's deepest desire for us to draw close to Him in our daily lives. He longs for His children's love and devotion.

James 4: 8 says, "Draw near to God and He will draw near to you." 1 Corinthians 6:19 tells us that our bodies are the temple of the Holy Spirit, which means God's presence by the Holy Spirit dwells within us. We draw near to God by opening ourselves to Him in worship, prayer and by simply spending time with Him. A lifestyle of worship, by its simplest definition, is positioning ourselves before God in acknowledgment of His sovereignty. It means daily communing with Jesus.

We need to spend regular time with God, where all that we are doing is focusing on Him. It is possible to live a life of experiencing God's presence with us wherever we go and whatever we do. As we live in this place, so we will find ourselves wanting to go deeper and developing our relationship with Him. It is vitally important for us to realize that God desires to speak with us. When we ask Him to speak to us. He will and we will become accustomed to hearing His voice clearly, distinctly and accurately.

As Proverbs 20:12 teaches us, God has created our physical ears and eyes and, in the same way, He has also created us with the ability to hear and see spiritually—our spiritual ears and eyes. It is important to realize that although we were created to hear His voice and to walk in communion with Him, it does take practice and experience to accurately discern the voice of God, each and every day. We must listen for His still, small voice above all the other noise that the world is bombarding us with on a daily basis. We must desire, discipline and delight in God's Word.

God has created us to have an intimate and meaningful relationship with Him. He longs to share His heart with us, to let us know His thoughts and His feelings. He is always available to us, and is always ready to act on our behalf.

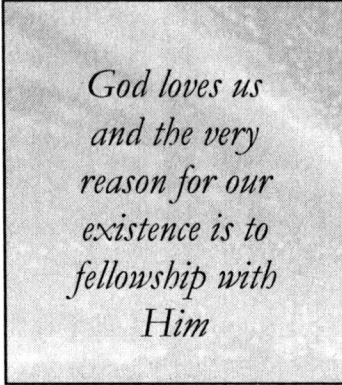

> *God loves us and the very reason for our existence is to fellowship with Him*

Becoming the Bride that Jesus is looking forward to marrying, only comes by us being transformed into His image. Jesus is the Bridegroom—the Lamb without blemish. Only by becoming like Him will we be ready as a Bride prepared for her Bridegroom. The following Scriptures will be an encouragement in your intimate relationship with the Lord.

And as the bridegroom rejoices over the bride, so shall your God rejoice over you (Isaiah 62:5b).

And the Spirit and the bride say, "Come!" And let him who hears say, "Come!" And let him who thirsts come. And whoever desires, let him take the water of life freely (Revelation 22:17).

God chose us to have fellowship with Him before the world was even formed. We need to walk in the understanding that God loves us and the very reason for our existence is to fellowship with Him.

It is comforting to know that God wants us to understand why we were created. His plan for mankind was never to create and abandon us. He is a loving Father—One who desires to share His plans and purposes with us so that we will be fully prepared and fully equipped to fulfill our destiny.

"I know the plans I have for you," declares the Lord. "Plans for welfare and not calamity and to give you a future and a hope" (Jeremiah 29:11).

Ministry should not be our priority in life, however worthwhile that ministry is. The development of any true ministry comes as we develop our relationship with God. As we draw aside from our busy lives and spend time with God, and ask Him to speak to us so we will hear His voice more and more clearly, He will develop our modes of communication with Him. From this place of intimacy, our ministries will develop and progress toward what God wants them to be—an outworking of our relationship with Him.

It is vital that we remain hungry for more and more of God. As Christians, we have two choices: we either keep pushing forward for more of God or we slide backward. There is no standing still.

We need to keep pressing forward, toward the prize that has been set before us, and not allow the things of this world to pull us back. If we are hungry for Him, He will meet that hunger in ways that we have not yet experienced. God is looking for those who are hungry for Him and He will reward them with His presence in greater ways than have been seen so far.

Jesus fervently desired to partake of that first communion with His followers. One day, He will drink of that cup once again with His Bride, as we celebrate together at the Marriage Supper of the Lamb. The Bridegroom is returning for a Bride without blemish. Let's make ourselves ready for our soon and coming King!

CHAPTER

9

THE BRIDE IS BEAUTIFUL

The Bride of Christ is a Loving & Beautiful Bride

There are many prophetic words being spoken about how the next move of the Spirit will be birthed out of this place of intimacy with God, with the overshadowing of God's Spirit in our lives. Psalm 91 declares, "He who dwells in the secret place of the Most High shall abide under the shadow of the Almighty." The shadow of God is the place where His glory covers every detail of our lives. It's a place of refuge and protection from all the plots of the evil one. It's also in the secret place where God infuses His strength and life into us continually.

As the presence of the Holy Spirit transcends His Church in this hour, there is coming an impartation to carry the seed of the next move of God. It is abiding in the secret place of intimacy with the Lord that is vitally important to receiving the fullness of all He wants to birth in the earth. It will be out of this place of abiding under His shadow that the creative force and power of His Spirit will be released in our lives, including the move of extraordinary signs, wonders and miracles. This demonstration of God's power through His people will be a direct result of the time spent in the secret place, under the shadow of His glory. We must guard our time with God and guard the seed He has placed in us. We cannot let the evil one snatch from our lives the things that would make us miss our divine appointed destiny. Out of the secret place of intimacy will come the release of life and power to see the glory of God, and it will cover the face of the earth as never before in this life time.

Gather the people, sanctify the congregation, Assemble the elders, gather the children and the nursing infants. Let the bridegroom come out of his room, And the bride out of her bridal chamber (Joel 2:16).

Let Him love you like you have never been loved before in life. It's so much simpler than we make it out to be. It's time to be transformed by His love, so that there is no fear in you.

There is no fear in love; but perfect love casteth out fear: because fear hath torment. He that feareth is not made perfect in love (1 John 4:18).

Be utterly abandoned in His love and in His Presence. God, in His glory, will pour and pour His presence into people to the degree that entire nations will be transformed. He wants to transform you with His love and He wants us to be conformed in His image. Nature forms us; sin deforms us, school informs us; but only Christ transforms us.

Out of the secret place of intimacy will come the release of life and power to see the glory of God

We are called to be carriers of His glory. It's not about standing up and being an eloquent speaker. It's about being so close to the heart of God that we know what He's thinking and we can feel His every heartbeat. Then we'll not be afraid to go anywhere and say anything. He captivates us so that we can never go back to our old and ordinary life. He wants to shatter our boxes and He wants us to be free from any hindrance that is obstructing our Bridal Love with the Lord. It is true that often our image of God is still too small. We must tell and show others how big our God is in our lives.

He changes us with one glance of His eyes, so that we are not afraid to be completely abandoned in His arms. Many want lots of power and anointing, but when you just lie down and let Him kill you, it's a good thing. He wants to love you to death. He wants to rid of you of anything that is blocking your affections toward Him. He's looking for union, not occasional worship, so that our nature is transformed. We must walk in His nature and we will die to our self daily.

There is going to be much grace given by God to get us where we need to be at the end of the age. We can't look, as Moses did, to our own inadequacy, which made the Lord angry, but to His adequacy to equip and lead the Bride to the fullness of what God will give the hungry heart in pursuit of Him.

All fruitfulness flows from intimacy. There is no other place to get it because to the degree that we are united with the heart of Jesus, God will bring fruit in our lives. It is to the degree that we are in love with Him that we will be fruitful. I have one message— passion and compassion. We're passionate lovers of God, so that we become absolutely nothing. His love fills us to His overflowing love and He changes us into His likeness. Jesus first forms us in our mother's womb, then He transforms us as His creation, so that He can conform us into the image of Himself.

There is an old story about a rich man who wished to buy a bride. He visited the village of his youth looking for a suitable mate. Many lovely young women tried to catch his eye, but they weren't quite what he had in mind.

Finally, to everyone's surprise he chose a maiden whom the villagers considered unattractive, certainly not wife material for an important, rich man.

The rich man went to the woman's father, who was happy that anyone would want his gangly daughter. The father suggested a dowry of one cow, but the rich man was appalled.

He told the astonished father that the young woman was much too beautiful to be purchased for only one cow and insisted on a bridal price of 100 cows. The two were married and it is said that the first gift the rich man gave his bride was a mirror, so she could look at her beauty.

A few years later the rich man and his wife once again visited the village. The people were shocked by the unbelievable loveliness of the wife and couldn't believe she was the same unattractive young woman who had once lived among them. But she was.

See, the woman had become the person her husband had seen all along, an incredible beauty. She had learned to see herself through his eyes and was transformed.[10]

Friend, you are the bride of Christ. Have you ever wondered if your Savior finds you attractive? Have you felt unworthy of His attention, uncomely, awkward, insignificant or ugly? Perhaps you're afraid to think about how Jesus views you. Maybe you're ashamed of your past or present behavior. Your faults spring up before you crying, "ugly, sinful soul." But the truth is that the Bride of Christ is beautiful. Words cannot describe how He sees you as His Bride.

She is clothed with the righteousness of Jesus. Despite her mistakes she has a tender heart after her Groom, one that longs to be loved. She looks toward Him with soft eyes like a dove's, desiring to please Him.

Scripture is quite clear about what Jesus sees when He looks at His bride. He says that she is beautiful, fair, lovely, and comely. He

10 Personal email. Unknown source

paid the highest dowry, offering His very life to purchase her. He knows about all that ugliness, but it was washed away in baptism and now His Bride stands before Him pure and radiant. And He is breathless as He experiences her beauty.

His heart is ravished for you. He sees the beauty in you and He is calling it forth. He's offering Himself to you, transforming you by His love. At the beginning of this book, it was mentioned that we are leaving the "Church age and entering now into the Bride age."

Jesus is lifting the mirror and asking you to seek a peek. How do you see yourself? How do you think others perceive your image? I do not know where that story originated from, but the Lord knows what you will find reflected in it. Radiant and transformed beauty is what you will find.

The Bride Belongs to the Bridegroom

What an intimate picture of Jesus' relationship with those He came to deliver! Jesus Christ wasn't merely a "messiah" or a "savior;" He came to re-establish with us the deep intimacy, communion, and passion that a husband and wife experience at their wedding. As Revelation 19:7 points out, we are being prepared as a Bride for the coming wedding and celebration feast when we meet Jesus, our Bridegroom, face-to-face. The breaking of the divine-human relationship that happened in the Garden of Eden is about to be reversed, re-creating an even greater intimacy than before, if we can fathom that perspective. The new creation of the Bride will surpass the original creation of the bride that was found in Eve in the garden of Eden.

Those who belong to Jesus make up His Bride. We are the ones He longs for, gazes upon, thinks about, and provides for. He is eager to sweep us up, away from the threats and opponents we often face. Like a young woman and her friends and family, we should be frantically preparing for that coming day, putting our affairs in order, collecting our wardrobe of righteous obedience, turning our hearts toward our Beloved, with whom we will be face-to-face in just a little while.

In this one brief prophetic exclamation, God speaks many things to us through John the Baptist, "The bride belongs to the bridegroom" (John 3:29). We must put off our modern notions and negative experiences, and appreciate afresh the unvarnished experience of marital love that portrays our relationship with Jesus as His Bride. Here are some brief points that are worthy of more full examination and understanding.

The Bridegroom picked us and chose us; we did not pick Him. We did not go to a certain website and put in our shopping list for our perfect love. No, while we were "dead in our sins," and without hope or thought to what we needed, He came and chose us. The more we learn about Him, the more we realize He is the One of our dreams. When we come to the wedding feast and stand before the risen Son, in whom the Father of Creation is well-pleased, we will truly know fulfillment of our deepest longings. Our knees won't be shaking because we wonder if we've made a mistake. Instead, a huge bell will be going off in the depths of our being, tolling "THIS is what, THIS is who, we have been longing and waiting for. Jesus the Risen One that fills the God-sized vacuum in us!"

Have you had a bad experience of marriage or of a wedding? Put that experience out of your mind because this will truly NOT be like anything you have every heard or experienced. Jesus is not like any other—this is a unique relationship. And this marriage supper will not disappoint us. All creation has been waiting for this party!

John, in his gospel, refers to himself as the disciple whom Jesus loved. He was part of the three disciples who were most intimate with Jesus. He was often described as being close by Jesus' side and even leaned on Jesus' breast (John 13:23). If we were that close to the Lord, we too would be assured of His love toward us. If one of the other disciples had a question to ask of Jesus, they would sometimes ask John to present it to Him (John 13:24-25). If we have that close and intimate relationship with Jesus and we lean on Jesus like John did, we would hear His heart-beat and know what He desires for us.

John loved Jesus passionately and he was aware of Jesus' love for him. By declaring himself "the disciple whom Jesus loved," John was in effect saying, "I know Jesus loves me." It was his understanding of Jesus' love for him that caused such a deep love to arise within his own heart. John acknowledges this in his first epistle: "We love, because He first loved us" (1 John 4:19).

This profound truth will be important for us to keep in mind as we walk with the Lord. As we see how great a source of motivation love is, we will naturally ask how we can be increased in love. The answer is that we must better understand how deeply Christ loves us. Love begets love. Passion begets passion. As we come to comprehend Christ's great love for us, we will find a reciprocal love arising within our own hearts toward Him.

> *As we come to comprehend Christ's great love for us, we will find a reciprocal love arising within our own hearts toward Him*

John made no rash vows, but, due to his deep love for Jesus, he remained as close as possible and so can we.

And Simon Peter was following Jesus, and so was another disciple. Now that disciple was known to the high priest, and entered with Jesus into the court of the high priest, but

Peter was standing at the door outside. So the other disciple, who was known to the high priest, went out and spoke to the doorkeeper, and brought in Peter (John 18:15-16).

John is speaking of himself here, as the other disciple known to the High Priest. He and Peter were the only two disciples mentioned as being near Jesus at his questioning before the High Priest. Unlike Peter, it was not discipline and determination that brought John in but it was because of love. He wanted to remain close to his beloved friend. It was impossible for him to be elsewhere. Many times, it can seem like discipline and determination that motivates us to decide to become close to the Lord and not just because we love Him.

At the crucifixion of Jesus, there were a number of women who followed Him, but only one of the twelve disciples. It was John. His heart of love would not allow him to be separated from his loving Master, even through a most unbearable time. At the crucifixion, Jesus committed two of the people who loved Him the most to one another—His mother and John.

When Jesus therefore saw His mother, and the disciple whom He loved standing nearby, He said to His mother, "Woman, behold, your son!" Then He said to the disciple, "Behold, your mother!" And from that hour the disciple took her into his own household (John 19:26-27).

I am certain that Mary never lacked anything while she was in John's household and under his care. John's care for her was due to his love for Jesus. In loving and caring for Mary, John was expressing his love. Love can be extravagant; it surpasses all other sources of motivation. Paul spoke to the Corinthian church of the excellence of love:

Love is patient, love is kind, and is not jealous; love does not brag and is not arrogant, does not act unbecomingly; it does not seek its own, is not provoked, does not take into account a wrong suffered, does not rejoice in unrighteousness, but rejoices with the truth; bears all things, believes all things, hopes all things, endures all things. Love never fails (1 Corinthians 13:4-8).

When, seemingly, will-power and determination failed Peter, love did not fail John. John was able to remain by Jesus' side, bearing and enduring all things, due to love. 1 Corinthians tells us that love does not brag, nor act arrogantly. It was not necessary for John to boast that he would never forsake Jesus because John was constrained and controlled by love. His actions would merely reflect his love for Christ. If only our actions, and not reactions, would reflect our intimate times with the Lord.

When Jesus was resurrected and the women reported the empty tomb, we are told that Peter and John raced to the tomb to inspect it.

And so she ran and came to Simon Peter, and to the other disciple whom Jesus loved, and said to them, "They have taken away the Lord out of the tomb, and we do not know where they have laid Him." Peter therefore went forth, and the other disciple, and they were going to the tomb. And the two were running together; and the other disciple ran ahead faster than Peter, and came to the tomb first; and stooping and looking in, he saw the linen wrappings lying there; but he did not go in.

Simon Peter therefore also came, following him, and entered the tomb; and he beheld the linen wrappings lying there, and the face-cloth, which had been on His head, not lying with the linen wrappings, but rolled up in a place by itself. So the other disciple who had first come to the tomb entered then also, and he saw and believed. For as yet they did not understand the Scripture, that He must rise again from the dead (John 20:2-9).

Here again, we see the excellence of love. We are told that when John looked into the tomb and he saw it empty, it was then that he believed. Peter merely marveled. Going back to Corinthians, we are told "love believes all things." It was love that allowed John to believe while others doubted.

It is in John 21 that we are told of another encounter between the disciples and Jesus after His resurrection. Peter decided to go fishing and the other disciples joined him. While they were a little ways from shore, Jesus called to them; the disciples did not know who He was. In this encounter, John recognized Jesus and it was he who told the other disciples, and it was only after John told them, that Peter recognized it was Jesus.

> That disciple therefore whom Jesus loved said to Peter, "It is the Lord." And so when Simon Peter heard that it was the Lord, he put his outer garment on for he was stripped for work, and threw himself into the sea (John 21:7).

Again, John's perceptiveness can be attributed to his love for his Lord. He was always hoping for an encounter with Jesus and was quick to believe. 1 Corinthians 13 tells us: "Love believes all things, love hopes all things."

Love is certainly an attribute of those who make up the Bride of Christ. Love is undoubtedly one of the greatest attributes. It will be impossible to embrace the cross and walk where Christ would have us walk without love. We will fail to believe, fail to hope, fail to endure, fail to bear all things, if we do not have love.

In the preceding examples, it would seem that God is striving to reveal a profound truth. Over and over, we see Peter and John facing the same tests, but with vastly different results. What Peter was unable to accomplish with human strength, will-power, and resolve, John accomplished with love.

I heard a pastor, who had performed many marriage ceremonies, state that he had never seen an unattractive bride. He said they were all made radiant by the love that was evident upon their faces and their face showed what was in their heart for their beloved. Even so, the most attractive feature of the Bride of Christ is her evident love for the Bridegroom. It is this love that allows her to advance where others will not go. It is this love that leads her from the Outer Court, through the Holy Place, into the Most Holy Place.

Those who are of the Bride have seen the joy that is set before them. This joy is in Jesus Christ. Jesus will also rejoice when we have adequately prepared to be His Bride. He is the passion and love of the Bride. He is her possession, her inheritance. His love for His Bride will keep her in readiness and in expectation of His appearing. Like John at the cross, she will not be able to be anywhere else but at His side. With a love that does not end, we too, must be at His side. Maranatha!

10

THE CULMINATION OF THE BRIDE

One of the distinctive characteristics of the Bride of Christ is that she is in surveillance or close watch for her Bridegroom at all times. She lives in anticipation for the culmination of the finale of the marriage supper of the Lamb. It will be an exciting time in the plan of God when this marriage is consummated, and it will be in the zenith when the culmination of the Bride happens.

Only Bridal love will keep her vigilant. The love that God, who first loved us, has poured into our hearts through the Holy Spirit will keep her on the alert. Being born of God, this love has within it the seed of divine life. It is immortal and indestructible and it never sleeps. And so the heart of the Bride of Christ is awake even when she sleeps.

Love is awake within the heart of the Bride of Jesus, no matter what darkness may surround her, no matter how great the danger of being overcome with sleep. This love is like a very sensitive instrument. A single string, plucked by the One she loves, sounds in her heart and immediately the Bride is awake. Rising quickly, she rushes to meet her Beloved. She would never miss those times when her Bridegroom draws near; for her, such encounters are a foretaste of heaven. So she will not sleep through the hour when the Bridegroom comes in glory to take His Bride to Himself and to celebrate with her the culmination of the marriage supper of the Lamb.

If you want to be a Bride of the Lamb, you must be ready to go out to meet the Bridegroom when He comes, and you must take care that this love is alive in you. Do not let it fade, but rather let it keep you spiritually alive and alert. Without this love, you will not be ready when He comes at midnight. Only if divine love burns in your heart can you awaken in a state of readiness, shaking off the paralyzing sleep that will overcome all humanity, believers and nonbelievers alike.

> *If you want to be a Bride of the Lamb, you must be ready to go out to meet the Bridegroom when He comes*

The midnight hour is almost here. The signs that Jesus spoke of, in Matthew 24, are being fulfilled in our day. Love is growing cold in so many in the Body of Christ. God's commandments are being widely rejected. The onward advancement of lawlessness is causing devastation, discouragement and despair. Blasphemy is on the rise, indicating a burning hatred of Jesus Christ. In many parts of the world, Christians are suffering for their faith and being persecuted for what they believe. We see that God's chosen people are returning to the land of their fathers, as part of prophecy being fulfilled. The Gospel is being preached through the world and especially through the world of Internet.

The Bridegroom is preparing to meet His own. But for whom will He open the door to the banqueting hall, where the marriage supper of the Lamb is to be celebrated on that glorious day of union between the heavenly Bridegroom and His Bride, when heaven resounds with the sound of singing and rejoicing? Those for whom love for Jesus is a way of life will see that door open.

In these exciting last days, we will see and experience holiness as one of the final steps in completing His cleansing work before presenting a Holy Bride to the Father. What is the Lord expecting for His Bride in these exciting last days? God is not calling His Church to re-evaluate its spirituality or doctrines, but He is asking us, as individuals, to become holy and change our own spiritual condition to become more like Him. A change for holiness can only be birthed out of an intimate relationship with Him.

Several times, I have mentioned that we are leaving the church age and beginning the bridal age in this hour. The Lord is looking for a type of holiness and intimacy that can only be experienced at the feet of Jesus in prayer and worship.

God is calling! The words you have read in this book will to help prepare you to be His Bride. God is preparing His Bride—His called out ones—for the wedding banquet of His Son, Jesus. It is a wedding feast that will take place just before the great judgments of God. This day is coming—in our lifetime!

Do you recognize that for 2,000 years, the Father has been preparing and making ready a wedding banquet for His Son! He is preparing a glorious bride for His Son—a bride wearing garments without spot or wrinkle. This is our great awakening and the beginning of the bridal preparation. The Bride of Christ is coming into her completeness as never before and we will glorify the Lord with our whole collective being. The "last days" Church – His "called out ones"—will exalt the Lord in praise, worship and dance!

A person that is concerned about holiness will strive to be like our Lord Jesus Christ. We will not only live the life of faith in Him and draw from Him daily peace and strength, but we will also labor to have the mind that is in Him and to be conformed to His image. It will be a desire to esteem all others better than ourselves. We will see more evil in our own heart than in any other in the world and will continually examine what is in our own mind, will and emotions. There is a desire to follow after spiritual mindedness in our walk with the Lord. We will endeavor to set our affections entirely on things above and cling to God's Word firmly, while we hold things on earth with a very loose hand.

May your eyes be opened and may your heart embrace the importance of being ready as a Bride of Christ for our soon-coming Bridegroom.

We must use the time that is left, wisely. We have the opportunity to open our hearts wide so that love for Jesus can flow in and shape our lives. Then, even while we sleep, this love is actively present —simply because our whole being is given over to Him. Do not tolerate anything that would diminish your love for Jesus and cause Him to withdraw His love from you.

We must decrease while the Lord increases in every activity and aspect of our lives. Do not tolerate a negative attitude toward any person. We must stay positive and be a light in a dark and sinful world. People will see the difference the Lord makes in our lives. Do not tolerate any false attachments to people or things because in this day and time, the attachments can become idols. Do not tolerate anything that would draw you away from Jesus' path of lowliness, poverty, disgrace, and obedience. Resist the temptation to go your own way, gratifying self. Be on your guard against losing the love you had at first. Holiness must be foremost in your life and in every part of it.

The hour is coming when the One whom your soul loves will appear, but you will not notice if you are not aglow with first love. Nor will you be drawn to Him, for only those who love Him with first love will be drawn to the Bridegroom. In that hour it will be too late to open your heart so that it may be filled afresh with love for Jesus, too late to buy the oil of love. Your heart must already be filled with this love. You must be a Bride with all your being so that He will receive you as such when He comes for His Bride. He will take as His Bride only those who loved Him ardently, even in the darkest moments, and who were ready because their lamps were filled with the oil of repentance and love. We must continually keep filled and not run short of that oil in that coming day of the Lord.

We have the privilege of being considered the Bride of Christ and that term is reserved only for Christians who attain extra oil. As oil represents a type of the Holy Spirit, having an extra measure of Him involves yielding to His influence every day to perform the appropriate works of God and successfully progressing through the sanctification process. The condition of yielding to the Spirit daily, is referred to as "blamelessness." This condition is motivated by a strong desire to patiently deal with all the hindrances that threaten to impede devotion to God. We have needed to find out why God symbolically used the depiction of marriage to communicate so many of His spiritual truths.

> *May your eyes be opened and may your heart embrace the importance of being ready as a Bride of Christ for our soon-coming Bridegroom*

The day of supreme happiness will be when Jesus celebrates the marriage supper of the Lamb with His Bride amid the rejoicing of heaven! It is worth sacrificing everything to gain bridal love, the pearl of great price, in order to know the joy of that day. Yet even if we were to give up everything in this life that is desirable and satisfying for body, soul, and spirit for the sake of this love, we would still have given too little. Attaining the supreme goal of the marriage supper of the Lamb is worth everything. Know that the midnight hour is approaching and with it the marriage supper of the Lamb. The Bridegroom is coming! Turn your back on everything that would hinder you from going to meet Him. We must live only to love Him as our Bridegroom.

The final Bridal Company will consist of those who have been purified. The Bride of Christ will have been stripped of all impurity. They have learned to follow the Lamb wherever He goes, as they have learned to recognize His voice amidst deafening chaos and confusion. They have consented to let God do that work in them, which results in them living for Him rather than for themselves. It is then we understand what it means to be without spot or wrinkle.

The death of self is that living sacrifice that we are all called to make. The death of self is the cross that must be picked up daily, in order to follow Jesus. This is a deeper and a much more difficult death to live out than the martyr's death. It is sometimes a painful process in order for us to be His glorious Bride.

This is the glorious, last-days Church, the Bride of Christ. She is clothed with God's fullness. She is founded upon the Lord Jesus Christ.

The coming of the Bridegroom is counter to our thought process in the West. In America, we have a culture that tells us the wedding is all about the bride. The bride picks her dress and her bridesmaid's dresses and she is at the center of all the activities, from walking down the isle to throwing her bouquet. The Jewish wedding ceremony is very different. Here, the engagement is set, the groom goes to "prepare a place" and then, at some point in the near future, he returns for his bride. His return is unannounced for the most part. The bride has to be ready to go with him. She is looking for him! Are you looking for Him? Are you asleep? Arise! Oh Bride, our Bridegroom is coming!

It is the experience we were made for and the experience that we will embrace forever. At the wedding supper of the Lamb and from that time on through eternity, our main identity is the Bride of Christ. Until then, we remain faithful to Him and say with all the redeemed of the Lord, "Come, Lord Jesus!"

> He which testifieth these things saith, "Surely I come quickly. Amen. Even so, come, Lord Jesus" (Revelation 22:20).

In closing, the words of a song written by Terry MacAlmon describe what is in my heart in regard to the culmination of the Bride. May we be ever ready for the Lord to come for His Beloved Bride.

Even So

Even so
Come Lord Jesus come
Even so
Take your bride away
How my soul
Longs to be with You, my Lord
Even so
Even so
Come Lord Jesus come[11]

---

11 Terry MacAlmon, *Even So.* Used by permission

To contact the author or order more books, please write:

Judith Moore
810 Donnelly Ave.
Columbia, MO   65203-2433
email – moore4Jesus@centurytel.net

You may also order more copies of *The Calling of the Bride* and other books from CSA Publishing at the XPmedia.com store.

BULK ORDERS: We have bulk/wholesale prices for stores and ministries. Please contact:
usaresource@xpmedia.com.

For Canadian bulk orders, contact:
resource@xpmedia.com
or call 250-765-9286.

CSA
PUBLISHING